Using Data *to*
Improve Learning
for All

Using Data *to* *Improve Learning* *for* All

A Collaborative Inquiry Approach

Nancy Love EDITOR

DEVELOPED AT TERC
CAMBRIDGE, MASSACHUSETTS

A JOINT PUBLICATION

This material is based on work supported by the National Science Foundation under Grant No. ESI-0541723. Any opinions, findings, and conclusions or recommendations expressed in this material are those of the author(s) and do not necessarily reflect the views of the National Science Foundation.

For information:

Corwin Press
A SAGE Company
2455 Teller Road
Thousand Oaks, California 91320
www.corwinpress.com

SAGE India Pvt. Ltd.
B 1/I 1 Mohan Cooperative Industrial Area
Mathura Road, New Delhi 110 044
India

SAGE Ltd.
1 Oliver's Yard
55 City Road
London EC1Y 1SP
United Kingdom

SAGE Asia-Pacific Pte. Ltd.
33 Pekin Street #02-01
Far East Square
Singapore 048763

Printed in the United States of America.

Library of Congress Cataloging-in-Publication Data

Using data to improve learning for all : a collaborative inquiry approach/
edited by Nancy Love.
    p. cm.
"A joint publication with National Staff Development Council and TERC and National Association of Elementary School Principals and Research for Better Teaching."
Includes bibliographical references and index.
ISBN 978-1-4129-6084-7 (cloth)
ISBN 978-1-4129-6085-4 (pbk.)
    1. Educational statistics. 2. Academic achievement—Data processing.
3. Curriculum planning—Data processing. 4. School improvement
programs—Data processing. I. Love, Nancy. II. National Staff Development
Council (U.S.) III. Technical Education Research Centers (U.S.)

LB2846.U85 2009
370.2'1—dc22   2008034484

This book is printed on acid-free paper.

08 09 10 11 12   10 9 8 7 6 5 4 3 2 1

Acquisitions Editor:	Dan Alpert
Editorial Assistant:	Megan Bedell
Production Editor:	Cassandra Margaret Seibel
Copy Editor:	Kathy Conde
Typesetter:	C&M Digitals (P) Ltd.
Proofreader:	Jennifer Gritt
Indexer:	Jean Casalegno
Cover Designer:	Scott Van Atta
Graphic Designer:	Brian Bello

Contents

Acknowledgments

Many people and organizations made this monograph possible. Funding was provided by the National Science Foundation (NSF), under Grant No. ESI-0541723. Special thanks to the monograph's champions at NSF, Janice Earle and Michael Haney. In addition, much of the research and development upon which this monograph is based grew out of another National Science Foundation project, the Using Data Project (ESI-0221415), a collaboration between TERC and WestEd, which piloted and field-tested the Using Data Process of Collaborative Inquiry, a focal point for this book. The main product of this project was a book by project staff Nancy Love, Katherine E. Stiles, Susan Mundry, and Kathryn DiRanna: *The Data Coach's Guide to Improving Learning for All Students: Unleashing the Power of Collaborative Inquiry*, published by Corwin Press (2008). Several chapters in this monograph draw on material from this guide, so we are especially grateful to Corwin Press and the guide's coauthors, who are, in effect, coauthors of this book.

This book also includes chapters coauthored by practitioners who implemented the Using Data Project's approach in their schools or districts, including Dr. David Timbs from Johnson County, Tennessee, and Lori Fulton, Thelma Davis, Janet Dukes, Greg Gusmerotti, and Joan Lombard from Clark County (Las Vegas), Nevada. Brenda CampbellJones and Franklin CampbellJones, participants in the Using Data Project's national field test, coauthored an important chapter on cultural proficiency and data use. We are grateful for their voices.

Many other schools, NSF projects, and individuals participated in piloting and field-testing the Using Data Process and contributed to the model, stories, and lessons described in this book. These projects and organizations include the Appalachian Rural Systemic Initiative Resource Collaborative at the University of Tennessee; the Arizona Rural Systemic Initiative at the American Indian Programs at Arizona State University Polytechnic in Mesa; the Clark County School District, Las Vegas, Nevada, and the Local Systemic Change Initiative, the Mathematics and Science Enhancement (MASE), K–5

Using Technology Project; East Tennessee Science Partnership, a Tennessee Math and Science Partnership Grant at the University of Tennessee; Johnson County (Tennessee) Schools; the K–12 Science Curriculum Dissemination Center at EDC, Newton, Massachusetts; the Stark County Mathematics and Science Partnership, Canton, Ohio; and a national field-test group of 35 education leaders. The contributions of Using Data Project evaluators John Zuman and Magda Raupp of the Intercultural Center for Research in Education in Arlington, Massachusetts, are also gratefully acknowledged.

Lori Likis served as the editor's close partner throughout the project, offering her able developmental editing and helping to shape the manuscript into a coherent book. Peggy Liversidge polished the document with her thorough and precise copyediting. Valerie Martin provided the graphic design. Several others at TERC helped to shepherd the project, including Dennis Bartels, Laurie Brennan, Mark Kaufman, Diana Nunnaley, Ann Rosebery, Glen Secor, and Beth Warren.

Finally, we are indebted to the editorial and production teams at Corwin Press. Dan Alpert was much more than our acquisitions editor. He was our champion, guide, and, above all, trusted friend. Megan Bedell, Cassandra Margaret Seibel, and Kathy Conde moved the project through production at lightning speed. Each of the individuals and organizations mentioned above, along with the valuable insights and encouragement from our reviewers, made this a better book.

PUBLISHER'S ACKNOWLEDGMENTS

Corwin Press gratefully acknowledges the contributions of the following reviewers:

Thelma Davis, Coordinator, K–5 Mathematics
Clark County School District, Las Vegas, NV

Jennifer Fischer-Mueller, Deputy Superintendent for Teaching and
    Learning
Brookline Public Schools, Brookline, MA

Tyrone L. Olverson, Principal
Waggoner Junior High School, Reynoldsburg, OH

Neva Rose, Project Director
Partnership for Reform in Science and Mathematics (PRISM), Atlanta, GA

About the Editor

Nancy Love is director of program development at Research for Better Teaching in Acton, Massachusetts, where she leads this education consulting group's research and development. She is the former director of the Using Data Project, a collaboration between TERC and WestEd, where she led the development of a comprehensive professional development program to improve teaching and learning through effective and collaborative use of school data. This program has produced significant gains in student achievement as well as increased collaboration and data use in schools across the country. Love has authored several books and articles on data use, including *The Data Coach's Guide to Improving Learning for All Students: Unleashing the Power of Collaborative Inquiry* (2008) with Katherine E. Stiles, Susan Mundry, and Kathryn DiRanna; *Using Data/ Getting Results: A Practical Guide to School Improvement in Mathematics and Science* (2002); and *Global Perspectives for Local Action: Using TIMSS to Improve U.S. Mathematics and Science Education* (2001) with Susan Mundry. She is also well known for her work in professional development as a seasoned and highly engaging presenter and author of articles and books, including *Designing Professional Development for Teachers of Science and Mathematics* (2nd ed., 2003) with Susan Loucks-Horsley, Katherine E. Stiles, Susan Mundry, and Peter Hewson. In 2006, she was awarded the prestigious Susan Loucks-Horsley Award from the National Staff Development Council in recognition of her significant national contribution to the field of staff development and to the efficacy of others.

Introduction

The purpose of this monograph is to make widely available vital lessons about how schools can use data effectively to meet the immediate and pressing need to improve results for students. We wrote it because we want our readers to turn the challenges of accountability into our greatest opportunity to prevent yet another generation of failure.

THE CHALLENGE AND THE OPPORTUNITY: MARSHALING DATA AS A FORCE FOR SCHOOL IMPROVEMENT

Despite decades of reform, achievement gaps[1] persist at the same time that accountability pressures and sanctions for failure are increasing. Schools know they *have* to improve. The question is *how*. Simply having more data available is not sufficient. Schools are drowning in data. The problem is marshaling data as the powerful force for change that they are.

Without a systemic process for using data effectively and collaboratively, many schools, particularly those serving high-poverty students, will languish in chronic low performance in mathematics, science, and other content areas—no matter what the pressures for accountability. Or even worse, abuses of data—drilling students on test items; narrowing the curriculum; tutoring "bubble" students while failing to improve instruction; instituting practices that further exclude, label, or discriminate against students of color—will leave underserved students even worse off. As Richard Elmore (2003) says, "When we bear down on testing without the reciprocal supply of capacity . . . we exacerbate the problem we are trying to fix" (p. 7).

---

[1] It is with ambivalence and because we are still searching for a better term that we use the phrase "achievement gap" throughout this book. Achievement gap refers to the differences in testing performance among student groups, but it fails to describe the legacy of exclusivity and institutional racism in the United States that contributes to these differences.

On the other hand, these very same conditions—widespread availability of data and the pressure to make use of them to improve results—create the possibility for immediate, dramatic, and permanent improvement in student learning and the closing of persistent achievement gaps. The research is unequivocal: When schools build collaborative cultures, commit to all students' learning, and use data systematically through ongoing inquiry into improving instruction, they improve results for students (Elmore, 2003; Loucks-Horsley, Love, Stiles, Mundry, & Hewson, 2003; Louis, Kruse, & Marks, 1996; Love, 2004; McLaughlin & Talbert, 2001; National Staff Development Council, 2001).

This monograph is about schools that are solving the problem of *how* to improve. The schools that inspired this monograph have close to doubled the percentage of African American students proficient in mathematics over a three-year period; virtually eliminated the achievement gap between students with disabilities and regular education students; cut the failure rate of Native American children in half; and steadily improved mathematics, science, and reading results for all children. It is not that these schools do not face daunting problems: historically low achievement (one school did not have a single student passing the state test a few years ago), lack of resources, poor attendance, high teacher turnover and student mobility, and more. But in the face of these, teachers have become problem solvers by putting data to work *for* students and applying the science of continuous improvement.

THE POWER OF COLLABORATIVE INQUIRY

The improving schools discussed in this book do not just throw data at teachers and say, "Now do better." They systematically prepare teachers to engage in collaborative inquiry, a process where teachers construct their understanding of student-learning problems and embrace and test out solutions together through rigorous use of data and reflective dialogue. They attend to teachers' ongoing professional learning in how to both understand and respond to data. Teachers learn not just to be data literate but to draw on deep knowledge of content and how to teach it and on an abiding belief in the capacity of all children to learn. Data Teams become vital centers of collaboration, meeting weekly to examine common and

> Using data to guide action is the most powerful lever we have to improve schools; and yet, despite the increasing quantity now available, data are woefully underutilized as a force for change.
>
> —Nancy Love, Katherine E. Stiles, Susan Mundry, and Kathryn DiRanna (2008, p. 16)

formative assessment data, improve their teaching, monitor results, and share their successes. Classrooms are transformed into living laboratories, alive with learning for both students and teachers.

When teachers are organized and prepared for engaging in ongoing collaborative inquiry, data assume their center-stage role in improving teaching and learning. They sound the alarm that someone is not learning and activate an immediate response. They stimulate dialogue about teaching, curriculum content, learning, race/ethnicity, class, and culture and challenge us to rethink our assumptions. They hold a mirror up to instructional practice and provide constant feedback to guide instructional improvement. In short, they become one of the most powerful levers we have for better serving all students.

Three Findings About Collaborative Inquiry

This monograph will introduce collaborative inquiry to you and highlight three important findings about it:

Collaborative inquiry continuously improves teaching and learning. The first finding is that collaborative inquiry has the power to solve the biggest problem confronting schools in the era of accountability: how to continuously improve teaching and learning. Unleashing the expertise and creativity of teachers, collaborative inquiry is truly one of the great, untapped resources for school improvement. You will see evidence of this in Chapter 1 in the discussion of results and in case studies in Chapters 5 and 6.

Collaborative inquiry requires wholesale cultural change. A second important finding is that collaborative inquiry is easier said than done; it requires wholesale cultural change in schools. Its foundation is a collaborative culture characterized by collective responsibility for student learning, commitment to equity (the right of all students to achieve at high levels), and trust. In the absence of such a culture, schools may be unable to respond effectively to the data they have. Chapter 1 describes this culture in more detail, and Chapters 2 and 3 provide more practical guidance about how to establish such a culture, while Chapters 5 and 6 paint a picture of what school culture looks like in schools where collaborative inquiry is thriving.

Collaborative inquiry is based on more than data. The third finding is that using data in itself, even in the context of collaborative inquiry, does not automatically improve teaching and learning. Improved teaching comes about when teachers implement sound teaching practices grounded in cultural proficiency—understanding and respect for their students' cultures—and a thorough understanding of the subject matter and how to teach it. Chapter 1 describes the core competencies for effective data use, and Chapter 4 elaborates on the critical importance of bringing a culturally proficient perspective to data use and collaborative inquiry.

AUDIENCE

This monograph is written primarily for school or district administrators and teachers who want to make more effective use of school data to continuously improve teaching and learning. It is also intended for anyone interested in school improvement, including department of education personnel, policymakers, boards of education, parents, higher-education faculty, and those providing professional development and other services to schools. It is relevant to any school—whether serving affluent or poor students, whether high- or low-performing—where any students are achieving at less than their capacity. Although our examples come mostly from mathematics and science education, the monograph is applicable to school improvement in any content area and at any grade level, K–12. Finally, the monograph's contents are geared to readers who are just embarking on establishing a high-performing, collaborative school culture as well as to those who are further down that road.

OUR GOALS

Our intention is for this monograph to

- help you turn the challenges of accountability into our greatest opportunity to prevent yet another generation of failure,
- act as a catalyst to dialogue and inquiry into how to use data to improve teaching and learning,
- inspire you with examples of schools that are improving.

We want to share with you what we have learned through experience about how to meet the challenges of accountability. Specifically, the book will

- articulate a theory of action, collaborative inquiry, and the essential, logically linked steps that connect data use to improved results for students;
- describe one model for school improvement, the Using Data Process of Collaborative Inquiry, which has been nationally piloted and field-tested with promising results;

- provide a rationale, conceptual framework, and practical tools for bringing a culturally proficient perspective to data use and collaborative inquiry;
- create vivid descriptions of collaborative inquiry in action, teasing out essential and broadly applicable elements of success;
- offer ideas and frameworks to expand your thinking about school improvement, data use, and equity.

THE USING DATA PROCESS OF COLLABORATIVE INQUIRY: THE GENESIS OF THIS MONOGRAPH

This monograph grew out of a three-year National Science Foundation–funded project, the Using Data Project, a collaboration between TERC and WestEd. The project set out to develop, pilot, and field-test a program, now known as the Using Data Process of Collaborative Inquiry, to provide educators with the skills, knowledge, and dispositions to put school data to work to improve teaching and learning. The goal of the project was to prepare education professionals to serve as Data Coaches, who would lead a process of collaborative inquiry with school-based teams and influence the culture of schools to be one in which data are used continuously, collaboratively, and effectively to improve teaching and learning.

Even the developers of the program, who had promised to improve student learning in their National Science Foundation grant proposal, were stunned by the results produced in schools implementing the Using Data Process: dramatic improvements in student learning and narrowing of achievement gaps as well as important changes in school culture. With their collective eighty years of school improvement experience, nothing project staff had done had ever made such a difference. The National Science Foundation supported this monograph as one vehicle for widely disseminating the findings from the project that could benefit the field. Another product of the grant, *The Data Coach's Guide to Improving Learning for All Students: Unleashing the Power of Collaborative Inquiry* (Love et al., 2008), is a step-by-step guide for implementing the Using Data Process with Data Teams. Chapters 1, 2, 3, and 6 of this monograph are largely based on material from this guide.

The editor and contributors to the monograph have had the chance to experience the power of the Using Data Process firsthand. They are the staff of the Using Data Project, professional developers who worked with diverse schools—urban, suburban, and rural, K–12—across the country to implement the Using Data Process. They are district leaders who created the conditions for successful implementation and teachers and administrators who brought collaborative inquiry to life in their own schools.

Finally, they are experts in cultural proficiency who helped Using Data Project staff and participating schools think about how to bring an equity lens to data, using it as a catalyst for constructive dialogue about cultural diversity and expanding opportunities for learning to underserved students. Through all of these authors' voices, the monograph draws out lessons that can accelerate the possibilities for data use in school improvement on a large scale.

ASSUMPTIONS INFORMING THIS MONOGRAPH

The following assumptions inform the perspective of this monograph:

Assumption 1. Making significant progress in improving student learning and closing achievement gaps is a moral responsibility and a real possibility in a relatively short amount of time—two to five years. It is not children's poverty or race or ethnic background that stands in the way of achievement; it is school practices and policies and the beliefs that underlie them that pose the biggest obstacles.

Assumption 2. Data have no meaning. Meaning is imposed through interpretation. Frames of reference—the way we see the world—influence the meaning we derive from data. Effective data users become aware of and critically examine their frames of reference and assumptions (Wellman & Lipton, 2004, pp. ix–xi). Conversely, data themselves can also be a catalyst to questioning assumptions and changing practices based on new ways of thinking.

Assumption 3. Data encompass much more than state test results. Data are all of the compelling evidence that grounds conclusions in actual results, not speculation. In this era of accountability, it is important not to rely on single and imperfect measures of student achievement as the basis for decision making about schools, instructional improvement, or students. It is equally important to "measure what we treasure," the rich array of knowledge and skills we want students to acquire to be productive global citizens, which often go beyond what is assessed on state tests. Appropriate uses of data call for educators to set meaningful goals for student learning and use multiple measures to assess progress toward those goals, including formative assessments, analysis of student work and thinking, disaggregated student-learning data, and data about instructional and school practices and perceptions. Collaborative inquiry is only as robust as the relevance, accuracy, fairness, variety, and reliability of the data in use.

Assumption 4. Every member of a collaborative school community can act as a leader, dramatically affecting the quality of relationships, the school culture, and student learning.

Assumption 5. When teachers learn and apply knowledge and skills linked to student-learning goals, students learn more. Ongoing, high-quality professional development that is part of the school day, guided by data, linked to teacher practice, and embedded in a professional community is the lifeblood of collaborative inquiry and school improvement.

HOW THE MONOGRAPH IS ORGANIZED

This monograph is divided into two sections. *Section 1: Collaborative Inquiry* includes Chapters 1 through 4. This section describes the soil in which effective uses of school data can grow: a high-performing collaborative culture characterized by ongoing collaborative inquiry to improve student learning. Readers will learn

- why such a culture is critical to linking data use to improved results,
- how to create the conditions for it to take hold,
- what kinds of data to use and how often,
- the salient features and stages of a model for collaborative inquiry,
- how to bring a culturally proficient perspective to data use and school improvement.

Chapter 1: Building a High-Performing Data Culture describes major shifts in leadership, collaboration, data use, instructional improvement, and school culture that take place as schools move toward collaborative inquiry and high performance. It highlights the role of the Data Coach, a school leader who is specially trained to guide collaborative inquiry. Together all these shifts comprise the theory of action for moving schools from resignation to high-powered uses of data and results.

Chapter 2: Getting Organized for Collaborative Inquiry discusses how school districts and individual schools seed the soil for successful implementation of collaborative inquiry. It answers the following practical questions: How can collaborative inquiry be integrated into your existing improvement efforts and with other initiatives? How do you build support among key people? Organize Data Teams? Select and prepare Data Coaches? Create time for collaboration? Ensure timely access to robust local data? Based on lessons learned through the Using Data Project, these are the conditions that can make or break the success of collaborative inquiry.

Chapter 3: The Using Data Process: A Model for Collaborative Inquiry describes the Using Data Process, the model for collaborative inquiry developed and field-tested through the Using Data Project. Like inquiry-based instruction in the classroom, collaborative inquiry works best, the developers learned, when teachers have a model to follow—a sequence of steps that guides the inquiry and helps to assure productive dialogue and results. The Using Data Process organizes collaborative inquiry into the following five stages: building the foundation, identifying a student-learning problem, verifying causes through use of research and local data about practice, generating solutions by drawing on research and using a Logic Model, and implementing solutions while monitoring implementation and results. This chapter provides the rationale and describes the essential features of each stage along with practical tools and real-life examples.

Chapter 4: Bringing Cultural Proficiency to Collaborative Inquiry contends that one of the most important things Data Teams can do is develop their knowledge and skills of cultural proficiency and apply them to their work. Authors Brenda CampbellJones, Franklin CampbellJones, and Nancy Love define cultural proficiency as a framework for expanding our notions of diversity, viewing our students' various cultures as a source of strength, and bringing an equity lens with these perspectives to data analysis. They offer practical tools for sharpening our equity lenses, including the Cultural Proficiency Continuum, which describes a range of responses an individual or organization might have to cultural differences.

Section 2: Stories From the Field brings in the voices of practitioners with two case studies:

Chapter 5: A District Uses Data to Improve Results: Johnson County, Tennessee, is the turn-around story of the Johnson County School District, a small, rural, and historically low-performing system with 75 percent of students on free-and-reduced lunch. Coauthored by Johnson County's former Supervisor of Instruction, Dr. David Timbs, this chapter brings to life the theory of action described in Chapter 1, tracing how this school system built the bridge between data and results. The case illuminates the role district leaders play in establishing the conditions to implement and sustain continuous improvement. It also draws out actions taken to dramatically improve the performance of students with special needs.

Chapter 6: A Data Team Problem Solves About Problem Solving: Clark County, Nevada, tells the story of one Data Team's application of the Using Data Process to tackle the problem of students' poor performance in mathematics problem solving. Written by teachers and administrators in Clark County, Nevada, this case follows the Katz Elementary School Data Team as they build their foundation, identify a student-learning problem, verify causes, and generate solutions to achieve results in mathematics problem solving. You will discover how the Data Team revised their initial explanations of their student-learning results by closely observing students as they engaged in mathematics problem solving. As a result, they took a different and more productive course of action.

Final Thoughts concludes the book by acknowledging the challenges of launching and sustaining collaborative inquiry in the face of the overwhelming and urgent demands already placed on educators. It suggests small steps that can be taken toward establishing a high-performing Using Data culture while keeping the larger goal in mind: for all of us to summon the courage and the love to search out and discover what we do not yet know about how to educate all of our children.

SUMMARY

The publication of this monograph comes at a critical juncture in education. Will the era of accountability engender greater resignation, cynicism, and failure? Or will it unleash the power of collaborative inquiry and the will to educate all children as an unstoppable force, moving us forward more quickly toward our goal of closing achievement gaps? It is our hope that you will use this monograph to inspire and inform your efforts to accomplish the latter.

REFERENCES

Elmore, R. F. (2003). A plea for strong practice. *Educational Leadership, 61*(3), 6–10.

Loucks-Horsley, S., Love, N., Stiles, K. E., Mundry, S., & Hewson, P. W. (2003). *Designing professional development for teachers of science and mathematics* (2nd ed.). Thousand Oaks, CA: Corwin.

Louis, K. S., Kruse, S., & Marks, H. (1996). Schoolwide professional community. In F. Newmann & Associates (Eds.), *Authentic achievement: Restructuring schools for intellectual quality* (pp. 179–203). San Francisco: Jossey-Bass.

Love, N. (2004). Taking data to new depths. *Journal of Staff Development, 25*(4), 22–26.

Love, N., Stiles, K. E., Mundry, S., & DiRanna, K. (2008). *The data coach's guide to improving learning for all students: Unleashing the power of collaborative inquiry.* Thousand Oaks, CA: Corwin.

McLaughlin, M. W., & Talbert, J. (2001). *Professional communities and the work of high school teaching.* Chicago: University of Chicago Press.

National Staff Development Council. (2001). *Standards for staff development.* Oxford, OH: Author.

Wellman, B., & Lipton, L. (2004). *Data-driven dialogue: A facilitator's guide to collaborative inquiry.* Sherman, CT: MiraVia.

Section 1

Collaborative Inquiry

1

Building a High-Performing Data Culture

By Nancy Love

Nancy Love is currently the director of Program Development at Research for Better Teaching in Acton, Massachusetts. She is the former director of the National Science Foundation–funded Using Data Project, a collaboration between TERC and WestEd that developed a professional development program to prepare science and mathematics educators to lead a process of collaborative inquiry with Data Teams and to influence the culture of schools to be one in which multiple data sources are used effectively, continuously, and collaboratively to improve teaching and learning. The project developed a structured approach to collaborative inquiry known as the Using Data Process, which is described in detail in Chapter 3. The product of the project is a book titled The Data Coach's Guide to Improving Learning for All Students: Unleashing the Power of Collaborative Inquiry, *available from Corwin Press (2008). This chapter is largely based on material from that guide and made available for this publication with permission from Corwin Press.*

Despite the endless pessimistic messages about the state of public education and the resignation many educators feel about high-stakes testing, we believe there is much to celebrate. Our purpose in this chapter

---

Based on material from *The Data Coach's Guide to Improving Learning for All Students: Unleashing the Power of Collaborative Inquiry* (2008) by Nancy Love, Katherine E. Stiles, Susan Mundry, and Kathryn DiRanna. Adapted with permission from Corwin Press.

is to bring to life how schools are overcoming resignation and producing results by unleashing the power of collaborative inquiry, a process where teachers work together to use multiple data sources to continuously improve teaching and learning.

Just as the inquiry process can make the classroom come alive with discovery, discourse, and deep learning, inquiry among teachers into improving student learning can breathe new life into schools and classrooms. Teachers possess tremendous knowledge, skill, and experience. Collaborative inquiry creates a structure for them to share that expertise with each other, discover what they are doing that is working and do more of it, and confront what isn't working and change it. It is the ongoing investigation into how to continuously improve student learning for more and more students, guided by the following simple questions:

- How are we doing?
- What are we doing well? How can we amplify our successes?
- Who isn't learning? Who aren't we serving? What aren't they learning?
- What in our practice could be causing that? How can we be sure?
- What can we do to improve? To deepen our knowledge of our content and how to teach it?
- How do we know if it worked?
- What do we do if they don't learn?

When teachers ask these kinds of questions, engage in dialogue, and make sense of data together, they develop a much deeper understanding of what is going on relative to student learning. They develop ownership of the problems that surface, seek out research and information on best practices, and adopt or invent and implement the solutions they generate. The research base on the link between collaborative, reflective practice of teachers and student learning is well established (Little, 1990; Louis, Kruse, & Marks, 1996; McLaughlin & Talbert, 2001). When teachers engage in ongoing collaborative inquiry focused on teaching and learning and make effective use of data, they improve results for students.

> *We couldn't wait to get our CRT [criterion-referenced test] results to see how much we had improved.*
>
> —Florence Barker, principal and Data Coach, Cartwright Elementary School, Las Vegas, Nevada

THE POWER OF COLLABORATIVE INQUIRY

As staff of the National Science Foundation–supported Using Data Project, we have seen the true power of collaborative inquiry, its potential to improve student learning, firsthand. We developed a model for collaborative inquiry known as the Using Data Process, along with the professional development program and materials to support its implementation, and piloted this approach in schools across the country. Project staff worked with schools that are serving among the poorest children in this country—children from Indian reservations in Arizona, the mountains of Appalachia in Tennessee, and large and midsize urban centers in the Midwest and West. A few years ago, some of these children were simply passing time in school with "word search" puzzles or other time fillers; some were permanently tracked in an educational system that doled out uninspired, repetitive curriculum. Some of the schools in which we worked had not a single student pass the state test, and most students were performing at the lowest proficiency level.

Collaborative Inquiry Improves Student Learning

Today, students in these schools have a more rigorous curriculum and are experiencing significant and continuous gains in local and state assessments in mathematics, science, and reading. For example, in Canton City, Ohio, all four middle schools, serving 66 to 82 percent poor students and 30 to 45 percent African American students, increased the percentage of students scoring proficient or above on the Sixth-Grade Ohio Proficiency Test in mathematics between 2002–03 and 2004–05. One school more than doubled the percentage (Ohio Department of Education, 2005b, 2005c, 2005d, 2005e). On the Ohio Seventh- and Eighth-Grade Achievement Tests, all student groups, including all racial groups, students with special needs, those receiving free-and-reduced lunch, and males and females, made gains (Ohio Department of Education, 2005a, 2006; see Figure 1.1).

The percentage of Canton City high school students earning proficient or above on the Tenth-Grade Ohio Graduation Test in mathematics increased by 25 percentage points from 2004 to 2006. As in Grades 7 and 8, all student groups made progress (Ohio Department of Education, 2006). For example, the percentage of African American students passing the Ohio Graduation Test in mathematics increased by 74 percent from 2004 to 2006 (Ohio Department of Education, 2006; see Figure 1.1).

In Johnson County, Tennessee, a poor, rural area with over 70 percent of students on free-and-reduced lunch, the schools exceeded the growth rates of some of the wealthiest and highest-performing districts on the state assessment. Most impressive were gains for students with disabilities. In Grades 3, 5, and 8, mathematics, the percentage proficient for this group increased from 36 to 74 percent from 2004 to 2006. In reading for the same grade levels, the percentage proficient increased from 54 to 70 percent, and in science, in Grades 3 through 6, from 60 to 73 percent (Tennessee

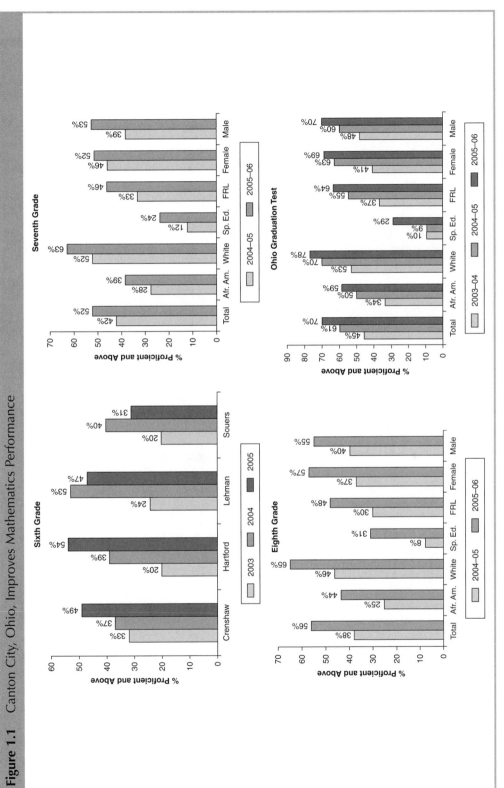

Figure 1.1 Canton City, Ohio, Improves Mathematics Performance

SOURCE: Data from Ohio Department of Education, 2003, 2005a, 2005b, 2005c, 2005d, 2005e, 2006. Figure from *The Data Coach's Guide to Improving Learning for All Students: Unleashing the Power of Collaborative Inquiry* (CD-ROM, Handout H1.3), by N. Love, K. E. Stiles, S. Mundry, and K. DiRanna, 2008, Thousand Oaks, CA: Corwin Press. Reprinted with permission of Corwin Press.

NOTE: FRL = Free and reduced lunch.

Figure 1.2 Johnson County, Tennessee, Improves Mathematics, Reading, and Science Performance

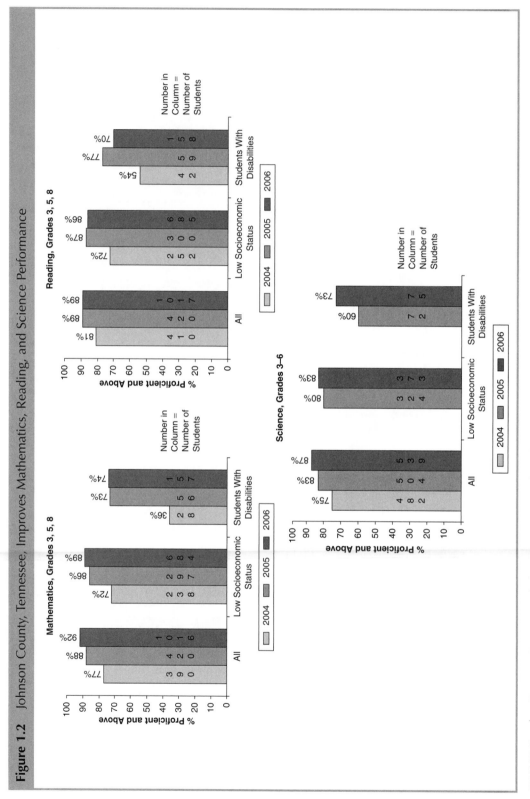

SOURCE: Data from Tennessee Department of Education, 2006. Figure from *The Data Coach's Guide to Improving Learning for All Students: Unleashing the Power of Collaborative Inquiry* (CD-ROM, Handout H1.3), by N. Love, K. E. Stiles, S. Mundry, and K. DiRanna, 2008, Thousand Oaks, CA: Corwin Press. Reprinted with permission of Corwin Press.

Department of Education, 2006; personal communication, David Timbs, February 21, 2007; see Figure 1.2).

Several of the schools participating in the Arizona Rural Systemic Initiative in Mesa, Arizona, serving a high percentage of Native American children, made substantial gains in student achievement on the Arizona State Assessment. For example, San Carlos Junior High School in San Carlos, Arizona, cut the percentage of students in the "Falls Far Below" category from 95 percent in 2002 to 46 percent in 2005 in eighth-grade mathematics and met Adequate Yearly Progress that same year (Arizona Department of Education, 2002, 2005).

Collaborative Inquiry Creates Data Cultures

Equally exciting, schools implementing collaborative inquiry not only improved student achievement on state tests and other local measures, they changed their school culture by increasing collaboration and reflection on practice among teachers. Teachers increased the frequency with which they used multiple data sources and engaged in Data-Driven Dialogue, and they made improvements in their teaching in response to data (Love, Stiles, Mundry, & DiRanna, 2008; Zuman, 2006). According to Using Data Project's external evaluators,

> *I don't think we can ever go back. Using Data has become a part of our culture.*
>
> —Mary Ann Wood, Data Coach,
> Salt River Elementary School,
> Mesa, Arizona

> As a result of UDP participation, many teachers have reported a significant shift in their [school] culture of using external factors to explain lack of student achievement. Many acknowledged that the process of discussing student test data has made them more accountable for the results and more mindful that teachers are in a position to influence gains in student outcome. (Zuman, 2006, p. 2)

Despite seemingly insurmountable barriers (e.g., limited resources, no common course or grade-level assessments, historically low performance), these schools managed to solve one of the biggest problems educators face: how to make effective use of the increasing amounts of school data now available to improve results for students.

BUILDING THE BRIDGE BETWEEN DATA AND RESULTS

Imagine two shores with an ocean in between. On one shore are data—the myriad data now inundating schools: state test data sliced and diced every which way, local assessments, demographic data, dropout rates,

Figure 1.3 Connecting Data to Results

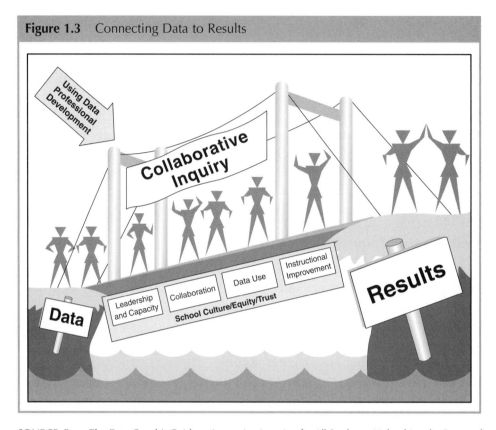

SOURCE: From *The Data Coach's Guide to Improving Learning for All Students: Unleashing the Power of Collaborative Inquiry* (p. 18), by N. Love, K. E. Stiles, S. Mundry, and K. DiRanna, 2008, Thousand Oaks, CA: Corwin Press. Reprinted with permission.

graduation rates, course-taking patterns, attendance data, survey data, and on and on. On the other shore are the desire, the intention, the moral commitment, and the mandate to improve student learning and close persistent achievement gaps. But there is no bridge between the shores with an ocean in between. What is often lacking is a process that enables schools to connect the data they have with the results they want. Sadly, it is children who are drowning in the data gap, particularly children of color, English language learners, children living in poverty, and those with exceptional needs.

Collaborative inquiry is the bridge that enables schools to connect the increasing amount of school data available to improve student learning. To implement collaborative inquiry, Using Data schools, that is, schools participating in the National Science Foundation–funded Using Data Project, set out to build the four segments that make up the bridge and the cultural foundation that supports it (see Figure 1.3).

> ### Establishing Collaborative Inquiry
>
> 1. Distribute leadership and capacity.
>
> 2. Build collaborative teams.
>
> 3. Use data frequently and in depth.
>
> 4. Focus on instructional improvement.
>
> 5. Nurture a collaborative culture based on commitment to equity and trust.

As collaborative inquiry grows, schools shift away from traditional data practices and toward those that build a high-performing Using Data culture. These shifts are summarized in Table 1.1 and elaborated on below.

1. Leadership and Capacity

The first segment of the bridge is building leadership and organizational capacity by equipping teachers and administrators with the requisite knowledge and skills to meet the challenges of accountability. It is important that these knowledge and skills are not just developed among formal leaders, but distributed among all members of the school community, especially teachers, who learn to act as leaders in improving student learning and influencing the school culture. As Michael Fullan (1993) points out, "Change is too important to leave to the experts" (p. 21). The problems schools face are simply too complex and ever-changing to leave improvement in the hands of few individual, charismatic leaders—no matter how skilled. Collaborative inquiry relies on every teacher becoming a change agent. When such leadership is widespread and institutionalized, with built-in mechanisms to sustain it, the result is organizational capacity. (See the Johnson County case study in Chapter 6 for a good example of how this is done.)

> *With increased accountability, American schools and those who work in them are being asked to do something new—to engage in systematic, continuous improvement in the quality of the educational experience of students and to subject themselves to the discipline of measuring their success by the metric of students' academic performance. Most people who currently work in public schools weren't hired to do this work, nor have they been adequately prepared to do it either by their professional education or by their prior experience in schools.*
>
> —Richard Elmore (2002, p. 5)

Table 1.1   Moving Toward a High-Performing Data Culture

Element	Less Emphasis On	More Emphasis On
Leadership and capacity	Individual charismatic leaders; data literacy as a specialty area for a few staff	Learning communities with many change agents; widespread data literacy among all staff
Collaboration	Teacher isolation; top down data-driven decision making; no time or structure provided for collaboration	Shared norms and values; ongoing Data-Driven Dialogue and collaborative inquiry; time and structure for collaboration
Data use	Used to punish or reward schools and sort students; rarely used by the school community to inform action	Used as feedback for continuous improvement and to serve students; frequent and in-depth use by entire school community
Instructional improvement	Individually determined curriculum, instruction, and assessment; learning left to chance	Aligned learning goals, instruction, and assessment; widespread application of research and best practice; systems in place to prevent failure
Culture	External accountability as driving force; focus on opportunities to learn for some	Internal responsibility as driving force; focus on opportunities to learn for all
Equity	Belief that only the "brightest" can achieve at high levels; talk about race and class is taboo; culturally destructive or color-blind responses to diversity	Belief that all children are capable of high levels of achievement; ongoing dialogue about race, class, and privilege; culturally proficient responses to diversity
Trust	Relationships based on mistrust and avoidance of important discussions	Relationships based on trust, candid talk, and openness

SOURCE: From *The Data Coach's Guide to Improving Learning for All Students: Unleashing the Power of Collaborative Inquiry* (p. 19), by N. Love, K. E. Stiles, S. Mundry, and K. DiRanna, 2008, Thousand Oaks, CA: Corwin Press. Reprinted with permission.

The key to leadership and organizational capacity in the Using Data Project was developing Data Coaches, education leaders such as teacher-leaders, instructional coaches, and building administrators who were specially trained to guide Data Teams through collaborative inquiry. Their role was to facilitate the work of Data Teams, helping them develop and apply critical knowledge and skills needed for effective use of data. While Data

Coaches played a crucial role in gathering and preparing data and keeping the work of Data Teams focused on improving teaching and learning, their role extended beyond individual Data Teams. Data Coaches became the agents of distributed leadership and a vital part of the permanent improvement of infrastructure that built organizational capacity. They helped to influence the school culture toward the elements of high performance described above and to sustain continuous improvement. One clear conclusion from the Using Data Project evaluation is that the leadership of Data Coaches was the key to successful implementation of collaborative inquiry (Zuman, 2006). (For more on the Data Coach's role, see Chapter 2.)

> **Data Coaches:** Educational leaders (teacher–leaders, instructional coaches, building administrators, or district staff) who guide Data Teams through the process of collaborative inquiry and influence the cultures of schools to be ones in which data are used continuously, collaboratively, and effectively to improve teaching and learning.

Core Competencies for High-Capacity Data Use

If leadership is to be widely distributed, what do all educators need to know and be able to do to use data well, engage in productive collaborative inquiry, and exercise their leadership in the service of improving student learning? In other words, what are the core competencies for high-capacity uses of data—those that translate into sustained and significant improvements in instruction and learning and act as the antidote to unproductive and even destructive uses of data that are widespread today? Through our work in the Using Data Project, we identified four knowledge bases on which effective leaders of collaborative inquiry draw (see Figure 1.4). These are the ability to

- apply data literacy and collaborative inquiry knowledge and skills to collect, accurately interpret, and analyze multiple data sources and research to identify student-learning problems, verify causes and generate solutions, test hypotheses, and improve results;
- apply content knowledge, generic pedagogical knowledge, and pedagogical content knowledge (how to teach a particular body of content based on understanding of student thinking, key ideas that comprise the discipline, and ways of making content accessible to students) to generate uses and responses to data that result in effective interventions and improved teaching and learning;

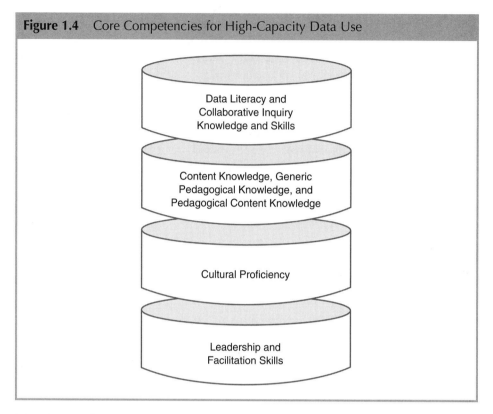

Figure 1.4 Core Competencies for High-Capacity Data Use

Data Literacy and
Collaborative Inquiry
Knowledge and Skills

Content Knowledge, Generic
Pedagogical Knowledge, and
Pedagogical Content Knowledge

Cultural Proficiency

Leadership and
Facilitation Skills

SOURCE: From *The Data Coach's Guide to Improving Learning for All Students: Unleashing the Power of Collaborative Inquiry* (p. 23), by N. Love, K. E. Stiles, S. Mundry, and K. DiRanna, 2008, Thousand Oaks, CA: Corwin Press. Reprinted with permission.

- apply cultural proficiency (the ability to interact knowledgeably and respectfully with people of diverse cultural backgrounds) to view achievement gaps as solvable problems, not inevitable consequences of students' backgrounds; generate solutions that reflect an understanding of diverse students' strengths, values, and perspectives; and handle cultural conflict effectively;
- apply leadership and facilitation skills to create high-functioning teams, facilitate productive dialogue focused on teaching and learning, foster commitment to rigorous content for all students, build collegial relationships based on trust and respect, and sustain collaborative inquiry.

2. Collaboration

The next segment of the bridge connecting data to results is collaboration. In Using Data schools, teachers were organized into collaborative Data Teams, generally of four to eight teachers and the building administrator or department chair, who worked together to use data to improve teaching and

Figure 1.5 A Data Team at Work

SOURCE: Courtesy of David Timbs, Johnson County Schools.

learning. At the elementary level, Data Teams were either grade-level teams or representatives of different grade levels who worked as content-area teams (e.g., mathematics or science) or as schoolwide improvement teams. At the middle or high school level, Data Teams were often organized by department or content area. However configured, Data Teams met regularly, ideally weekly during the school day.

> **Data Teams:** Teams of four to eight teachers, other school faculty, and ideally, their building administrator who work together to use data to improve student learning.

Data Teams used data frequently and in depth to guide instructional improvement. The most successful Using Data schools put in place benchmark common assessments and engaged teachers in regular analysis of item-level data and student work to identify and address student-learning problems (see data pyramid in Figure 1.6). They learned to stop blaming students and their circumstances

Using data used to mean rubbing teachers' noses in poor performance. But that didn't get us anywhere. Now we have a process that gives teachers a voice and a lens for looking at data. With teachers as the change agents, we are starting to see real movement.

—Richard Dinko, former coprincipal investigator, Stark County Mathematics and Science Partnership, Canton, Ohio

Figure 1.6 The Data Pyramid

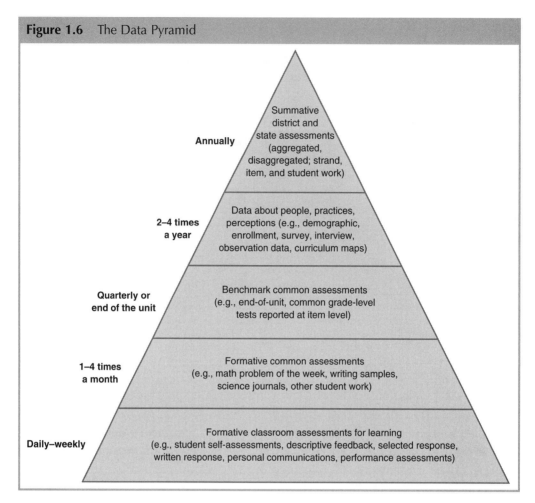

SOURCE: From *The Data Coach's Guide to Improving Learning for All Students: Unleashing the Power of Collaborative Inquiry* (p. 129), by N. Love, K. E. Stiles, S. Mundry, and K. DiRanna, 2008, Thousand Oaks, CA: Corwin Press. Reprinted with permission.

for failure and, instead, to use research and data about their instructional practice to generate solutions to identified gaps in student learning. Data Teams tried out new teaching strategies, such as use of graphing calculators, graphic organizers, or high-level questioning. They implemented new programs, such as maximum inclusion for students with disabilities, implementation of inquiry-based science instructional materials, and use of school-based instructional coaches. And they frequently monitored results. (See vignette that follows in this chapter for an example of a Data Team in action and Chapter 2 for more information on the role of the Data Team.)

3. Data Use

Let's focus further on the "data use" segment of the bridge. The days of using data in schools once a year are over. If continuous improvement is the goal, there is little point in examining only one source of data, state test results, which often become available only after students have moved on to the next grade and it is too late to do anything about them. Data-literate teachers use a variety of different kinds of data, some on a daily basis, some monthly or quarterly, and some annually, to continuously improve instruction and engage in collaborative inquiry. These include both formative and summative assessments. Formative assessments are assessments *for* learning and happen while learning is still under way and throughout teaching and learning to diagnose needs, plan next steps, and provide students with feedback. Summative assessments are assessments *of* learning and happen after learning is supposed to have occurred to determine if it did (Stiggins,

> *Teachers didn't know how to talk about data. It was at a surface level. It wasn't going down deep. Now we go into great detail.*
>
> —Keith Greer, principal,
> Casa Grande High School,
> Casa Grande, Arizona
>
> *We talked about standards. But it wasn't until we implemented common benchmark assessments that our teachers started teaching to the standards.*
>
> —Pam Bernabei-Rorrer,
> mathematics and Data Coach,
> Canton City, Ohio

Arter, Chappuis, & Chappuis, 2004, p. 31). Figure 1.6 illustrates the different types of data recommended for use by Data Teams, including formative, summative, and other kinds of data, with suggestions for the frequency with which those data are analyzed.

Formative Classroom Assessment Data. The widest part of the pyramid, at the bottom, illustrates the type of data that we suggest teachers spend the bulk of their time using—formative classroom assessments, done by teachers in their classrooms on an ongoing basis, including student self-assessments, descriptive feedback to students, use of rubrics with students, multiple methods of checking for understanding, and examination of student work such as science journals as well as tests and quizzes. These data inform teachers' instructional decisions—day-to-day, even minute-by-minute— and serve as the basis for feedback to students to help them improve their learning. For example, in Canton City, Ohio, middle school mathematics teachers use handheld electronic devices, Texas Instruments Navigator™ and graphing calculators, with their students to quickly assess student understanding of lessons while they are in progress. They then use this information to adjust their teaching, give specific feedback to students, and provide extra help for students who need it. Because of the strong research base indicating that these types of assessments improve student learning, we recommend that individual teachers spend the bulk of their data-analysis time developing, collecting, and analyzing these data (Black, 2003; Black & Wiliam, 1998; Bloom, 1984; Meisels et al., 2003; Rodriguez, 2004; Stiggins et al., 2004).

Formative Common Assessment Data. The next layer of the data pyramid represents formative common assessments, which are frequently analyzed by the Data Team—one to four times per month. These include some of the same sources of data as the formative classroom assessments, the difference being that teams of teachers administer these assessments together and analyze them in their Data Teams. For example, teachers meet weekly to examine student entries in their science journals and brainstorm ideas for improving instruction. These formative common assessments are important in identifying student-learning problems, generating short cycles of improvement, and frequently monitoring progress toward the overall student-learning goal.

Benchmark Common Assessment Data. The next layer of the data pyramid illustrates benchmark common assessments, administered at the end of a unit or quarterly to assess to what extent students have mastered the concepts and skills in the part of the curriculum recently taught. These are administered together by teachers teaching the same content, either at the same grade level or in the same subject or course. The "common" feature makes them an ideal source of data for collaborative inquiry. In fact, they are among the most important sources of student-learning data the team has because they are timely, closely aligned with local curriculum, and available to teachers at the item level (i.e., results are reported on each individual item and the items themselves are available for the teachers' examination). Benchmark common assessments are most effective when they include robust performance tasks that provide evidence of student thinking and when multiple-choice items are analyzed item-by-item to uncover patterns in student choices and confusion underlying incorrect answer choices.

Benchmark common assessments can be used both formatively, to immediately improve instruction, and summatively, to inform programmatic changes in the future, such as increasing the amount of time spent on teaching a particular concept or changing the sequence in which it is taught. Whether developed by the team, included in curriculum materials, or purchased commercially, it is crucial that these tests are of high quality—valid (measure what is intended), reliable (would produce a similar result if administered again), and as free of cultural bias as possible.

Data About People, Practices, and Perceptions. The next layer in the data pyramid, data about people, practices, and perceptions, is one that is often overlooked in schools, but it is extremely important. This type of data includes demographic data about student populations, teacher characteristics, course enrollment, and dropout rates. The Data Team analyzes demographic data to understand who the people are that comprise the school community. This slice of data also includes student enrollment in various types and levels of courses, such as in higher-level mathematics and science or advanced placement courses, and survey, observation, and interview data, which provide critical information about instructional practices, policies, and perceptions of teachers, students, administrators, and parents. These data become very important in exploring systemic causes of the student-learning problem identified through student-learning data, expanding opportunities for more students to learn, and monitoring implementation. They also help to assure that diverse voices—by role (e.g., student, teacher, parent, administrator), by race/ethnicity, and by economic, language, and educational status—are brought into the work of the Data Team. We recommend that Data Teams make use of these types of data two to four times per year to establish baseline data and monitor changes in practice.

Summative Assessment Data. The top of the data pyramid represents summative assessment data, including state assessments as well as annual district tests. These data are used to determine if student outcomes have been met and for accountability purposes. Data Teams take full advantage of these data, drilling down into them and analyzing them in as much detail as possible, including aggregated (largest group level) and disaggregated (broken out by student populations, e.g., race/ethnicity, gender, poverty, language, mobility, and educational status) data trends, strand (content domains), item-level data (student performance on each individual test item), and student work when available. Along with other student-learning data sources described above, they become the basis for identifying a student-learning problem and setting annual improvement targets. However, they occupy a small part of the pyramid because they are only available annually and provide limited information about what to do to improve performance (especially if item-level data and released items are not available). In addition, these results often arrive too late for teachers who taught a group of students during the year of the test to respond to them. Finally, these tests can be poorly constructed, culturally biased, inaccurate in content, and lacking in rigor, underscoring the importance of using the rich array of data recommended in the data pyramid.

Vignette

Using Multiple Data Sources to Improve Student Graphing Skills

The following illustrative vignette shows how an eighth-grade science Data Team drew on state assessment data and open-assessment prompts as well as on national and state standards and misconceptions research to improve students' graphing skills.

The analysis of the eighth-grade criterion-referenced test science strand data for "investigation and experimentation" indicated that only 42 percent of the students scored at the proficient level. Item-level data revealed that three questions about plotting and interpreting graphs had the lowest percentage of correct answers. Even with this drill-down, the Data Team was left with lingering questions about why students were not able to answer these questions. It was evident to the team that analyzing only multiple-choice questions would not help them understand students' naive or alternate conceptions about graphing. The teachers knew that in order to enhance their instruction, they needed to know exactly the concepts or content students were struggling to master.

The Data Coach brought the national and state science standards to the table for discussion. Using the documents helped the team to clarify their own content knowledge and build a common understanding of what eighth-grade students should know about charting, graphing, and summary statements. The list of concepts included (1) appropriate graphic representation (e.g., bar, line, pie), (2) orientation of x- and y-axes, (3) parallel and perpendicular lines, (4) labeling of manipulated (independent) variables and responding (dependent) variables, and (5) analysis of the relationship of manipulated and responding variables.

The team also discussed their experiences with teaching graphing and where students seemed to "always struggle." Reviewing misconception research helped the team confirm that two of the most common misconceptions involved use of appropriate graphs to display the data and understanding the relationship between the variables.

This discussion piqued their interest. What could they do to gather student work on this subject? The team decided to create an open-ended assessment prompt that asked students to graph data from a table that clearly labeled the variables and to make a summary statement from the graphic representation. They asked all eighth-grade science teachers to randomly select ten students in their classes to take the open-ended assessment. This resulted in fifty pieces of student work, such as the one illustrated in Figure 1.7.

To interpret the student work, the Data Team invited all teachers who gave the assessment to join in the analysis. First the teachers reviewed the scoring criteria (rubric) for expected student answers. Then they sorted the work into high-, medium-, and low-quality piles based on the scoring criteria and discussed the characteristics of each group. How was student understanding represented in the high-quality pile? What was lacking in a student's knowledge that indicated an intermediate level of understanding? What types of instructional interventions would be necessary to move a student from the low-quality to the medium-quality pile?

To answer these questions, they began by making the following observations of the student work, without any interpretation or inference:

- Paper A uses a bar graph rather than a line graph.
- Papers A, B, and D have no title.
- Papers A and B have mixed up the variables, plotting the manipulated variable (ground temperature) on the y-axis instead of the x-axis.
- Most data points are plotted correctly.
- Papers A, B, and C don't use data from the graph to explain the changes, although they do state the change (colder temperature, taller plants).
- Paper D has a wrong relationship (warmer ground, taller plants).
- Paper E is the only one to use actual data numbers.

These rich discussions resulted in the team documenting the following inference about student understanding: students have difficulty understanding the difference between when to use a bar graph (discontinuous data) and a line graph (continuous data). They are also not using data as evidence when writing a summary statement of the data.

Figure 1.7 Student Work Example

Open-Ended Prompt

Please write (or draw) your answer directly on the lines or in the space provided.

- You are the owner of a company that supplies local florists with tulips. Last year the tulips you produced tended to be smaller than usual and you wonder if it had something to do with the soil temperature in the winter.
- You recorded the ground temperature where the tulip bulbs were dormant and the average height of the plants when they sprouted. Your data chart looks like this:

HEIGHT OF TULIP PLANTS
ONE WEEK AFTER BREAKING THROUGH SOIL

	AREA A	AREA B	AREA C
Ground Temperature in Winter	7 C	2 C	0 C
Average Height of Plants	4 cm	8 cm	14 cm

1. Graph the data on the grid below. Remember to label the graph.

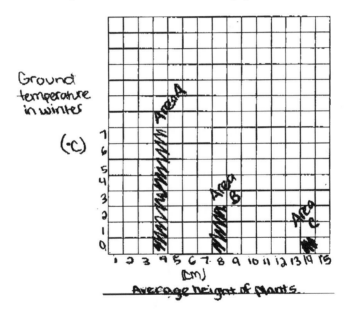

Ground temperature in winter (°C)

Average height of plants (cm)

2. Based on the data from the graph, describe the relationship between ground temperature in winter and the height of tulip plants after a week of visible growth.

   The relationship is the more the temperature goes
   down the height gets taller.

SOURCE: Adapted from the Fall 2004 Partnership for Student Success in Science student assessment. Designed by Dr. Shavelson of Stanford University. Reprinted with permission.

NOTE: This figure is also used in *The Data Coach's Guide to Improving Learning for All Students: Unleashing the Power of Collaborative Inquiry* (p. 219), by N. Love, K. E. Stiles, S. Mundry, and K. DiRanna, 2008, Thousand Oaks, CA: Corwin Press.

This led to a discussion of how graphing was taught. It soon was apparent that the mathematics and science teachers as a group were not articulating their content or their strategies. It was also clear that there were no common criteria for a quality graph or summary statements for Grades 6 through 8. The team set out to implement the following changes: (1) meet with mathematics teachers to articulate content and strategies, (2) develop common criteria for quality graphing across content areas, (3) teach the students the criteria, (4) collect and analyze student work on graphing on a monthly basis, and (5) give students specific feedback on how to improve. They were excited when their new samples of student work showed more students meeting the criteria for success.

SOURCE: From *The Data Coach's Guide to Improving Learning for All Students: Unleashing the Power of Collaborative Inquiry* (pp. 218–220), by N. Love, K. E. Stiles, S. Mundry, and K. DiRanna, 2008, Thousand Oaks, CA: Corwin Press. Reprinted with permission.

4. Instructional Improvement

The driving purpose for collecting all of the data described above is instructional improvement. There is no way to bridge the gap between data and results without changing what is taught, how it is taught, and how it is assessed. Instructional improvement is the last and essential segment of the bridge linking data to results. The above vignette illustrates several important features of using data for instructional improvement:

- Keep the conversation focused on improving instruction, and establish ground rules for not blaming students, their circumstances, other teachers, or factors outside of their control.
- Use multiple data sources, including state and local test data at the strand and item level to identify the specific knowledge and skills students may be having difficulty with.
- Use national and local standards and misconceptions research to deepen teachers' content knowledge about the particular content or skill students are struggling with, thereby enhancing teachers' ability to analyze the work for student thinking and misconceptions.
- Collect student work that will further elucidate student understanding relative to the learning problem being investigated.
- Clarify what quality student work looks like, using anchor papers and exemplars.
- When analyzing student work and other data, separate observations from inferences and further test inferences with additional data and research.
- When generating inferences, use the following questions to guide the dialogue:
  - Are our learning goals, instruction, and assessment aligned?
  - Did we teach this concept/skill? Did we teach it in enough depth? At the appropriate development level? In the best sequence?

- Did we use appropriate and varied instructional strategies to meet each student's needs?
- Did we use quality questions to extend student thinking?
- Did we use formative assessment data to give students feedback on their own learning and to identify student confusion and refocus our teaching?
- Did all students have access to this content and best practice?
- What content knowledge and pedagogical content knowledge will strengthen our ability to teach this content?
- Did we apply principles of cultural proficiency (knowledge and respect for people from diverse cultural backgrounds) to assure the best learning opportunities for culturally diverse learners?

• Use additional data (e.g., student and teacher surveys, classroom observations, student and teacher interviews, and student enrollment in advanced courses) and research to verify the causes of the student-learning problem and generate research-based solutions.

• Test solutions through ongoing monitoring of student learning in the problem area identified.

5. Collaborative Culture

As illustrated in Figure 1.3, the foundation of the bridge of collaborative inquiry is a school culture characterized by collective responsibility for student learning and the commitment to serve each and every child. Long before state tests, plenty of cues and data were available to let us know some students were not learning—students slumping down in their seats, going through day after day of school without being engaged, poor grades, poor attendance, high dropout rates. Educators working in isolation, however, literally could not respond to the data. Yet the addition of accountability testing also does not assure the ability to respond to data, or "response-ability." This is a function of a collaborative culture, where everyone takes responsibility and is committed to improving learning for all students. Schools that have response-ability do not leave student learning to chance. As Rick DuFour and his colleagues (DuFour, DuFour, Eaker, & Karhanek, 2004) describe it, they "create a schoolwide system of interventions that provides all students with additional time and support when

When people here say "data," they usually think of that stuff they take care of in the office. Through the Using Data Project, we learn that we work together to analyze the data and that there are direct implications for classroom instruction. There is something that everyone can do to have all of our students be the best they can be.

—Karen Croteau, Data Coach and teacher, Clark County School District, Las Vegas, Nevada they experience initial difficulty in their learning" (p. 7). High-performing collaborative schools are organized in grade-level or course- or subject-based teams where this response-ability is enacted as part of the daily work of teachers.

A hallmark of such a high-performing school culture is a commitment to equity. Singleton and Linton (2006) define educational equity as "raising the achievement of all students while narrowing the gap between the highest- and lowest-performing students and eliminating the racial predictability and disproportionality of which student groups occupy the highest and lowest achievement categories" (p. 46). Equity does not mean that all students receive an equal level of resources and support, but that those with the greatest need receive the level of support they need to succeed.

A collaborative community committed to equity requires a high level of trust. In high-functioning school cultures, educators trust each other enough to discuss "undiscussables" such as race, reveal their own practices and mistakes, root for one another, and face together the brutal facts that data often reveal (Barth, 2006). For all of these reasons, districts that want to unleash the power of collaborative inquiry make a top priority of strengthening collaboration and internal responsibility for student learning, commitment to equity, and relationships based on trust. Collaborative inquiry both thrives in such a culture and helps to establish it. (See Chapter 3 and the case studies in Chapters 5 and 6 for more on how Data Teams and Data Coaches build the foundation for collaborative inquiry.)

SUMMARY

How do schools go from simply having data to actually producing results for students by skillful use of that data? In this monograph the authors present a process that enables schools to connect the data that they have to the results they want. This process is collaborative inquiry—where teachers work together to construct their understanding of student-learning problems and embrace and test out solutions together through rigorous use of data and constructive dialogue. It acts as the bridge between data and results. The Using Data Process, described in detail in Chapter 3, provides one model of collaborative inquiry with demonstrated results for students.

As learned through implementation of the Using Data Process, building the bridge is not easy. It requires major changes in how schools do business, starting with a shift away from individual change agents and toward distributed leadership. The Data Coach is the agent for distributing leadership, guiding Data Teams, and developing members' knowledge and skills in the four core competencies upon which the effective use of data depends:

1. Data literacy and collaborative inquiry knowledge and skills

2. Content knowledge, generic pedagogical knowledge, and pedagogical content knowledge

3. Cultural proficiency

4. Leadership and facilitation skills

Other building blocks of the bridge are collaboration, put into practice by organizing teachers into Data Teams or professional learning communities; frequent and in-depth use of multiple data sources; and ongoing instructional improvement. The foundation for the bridge—upon which all of these elements rest—is a collaborative culture characterized by trust and a commitment to every student's learning.

REFERENCES

Arizona Department of Education. (2002). *Arizona school report card: San Carlos Junior High School.* Retrieved June 13, 2006, from http://www.ade.az.gov/srcs/ReportCards/48632003.pdf

Arizona Department of Education. (2005). *Arizona school report card: San Carlos Junior High School.* Retrieved June 13, 2006, from http://www.ade.az.gov/srcs/ReportCards/48632006.pdf

Barth, R. (2006). Improving relationships within the schoolhouse. *Educational Leadership, 63*(6), 8–13.

Black, P. (2003, April). *A successful intervention—Why did it work?* Paper presented at American Educational Research Association annual meeting, Chicago.

Black, P., & Wiliam, D. (1998). Inside the black box: Raising standards through classroom assessment. *Phi Delta Kappan, 80*(2), 139–148.

Bloom, B. S. (1984). The search for methods of group instruction as effective as one-to-one tutoring. *Educational Leadership, 41*(8), 4–17.

DuFour, R., DuFour, R., Eaker, R., & Karhanek, G. (2004). *Whatever it takes: How professional learning communities respond when kids don't learn.* Bloomington, IN: National Educational Service.

Elmore, R. F. (2002). *Bridging the gap between standards and achievement: The imperative for professional development in education.* Washington, DC: Albert Shanker Institute.

Fullan, M. (1993). *Change forces: Probing the depths of educational reform.* London: Falmer.

Little, J. W. (1990). Teachers as colleagues. In A. Lieberman (Ed.), *Schools as collaborative cultures: Creating the future now* (pp. 165–193). New York: Palmer.

Louis, K. S., Kruse, S., & Marks, H. (1996). Schoolwide professional community. In F. Newmann & Associates (Eds.), *Authentic achievement: Restructuring schools for intellectual quality* (pp. 179–203). San Francisco: Jossey-Bass.

Love, N., Stiles, K. E., Mundry, S., & DiRanna, K. (2008). *The data coach's guide to improving learning for all students: Unleashing the power of collaborative inquiry.* Thousand Oaks, CA: Corwin Press.

McLaughlin, M. W., & Talbert, J. (2001). *Professional communities and the work of high school teaching.* Chicago: University of Chicago Press.

Meisels, S. J., Atkins-Burnett, S., Xue, Y., Nicholson, J., Bickel, D. D., & Son, S.-H. (2003). Creating a system of accountability: The impact of instructional assessment on elementary children's achievement test scores. *Education Policy Analysis Archives, 11*(9). Retrieved June 14, 2006, from http://epaa.asu.edu/epaa/v11n9/

Ohio Department of Education. (2003). *Canton City School District 2002–2003 school year report card.* Retrieved August 6, 2007, from http://www.ode.state.oh.us/reportcardfiles/2002–2003/DIST/043711.pdf

Ohio Department of Education. (2005a). *Canton 2004–2005 school year report card.* Retrieved August 6, 2007, from http://www.ode.state.oh.us/reportcardfiles/2004–2005/DIST/043711.pdf

Ohio Department of Education. (2005b). *Crenshaw Middle School 2004–2005 school year report card.* Retrieved August 6, 2007, from http://www.ode.state.oh.us/reportcardfiles/2004–2005/BUILD/065508.pdf

Ohio Department of Education. (2005c). *Hartford Middle School 2004–2005 school year report card.* Retrieved August 6, 2007, from http://www.ode.state.oh.us/reportcardfiles/2004–2005/BUILD/015495.pdf

Ohio Department of Education. (2005d). *Lehman Middle School 2004–2005 school year report card.* Retrieved August 6, 2007, from http://www.ode.state.oh.us/reportcardfiles/2004–2005/BUILD/020123.pdf

Ohio Department of Education. (2005e). *Souers Middle School 2004–2005 school year report card.* Retrieved August 6, 2007, from http://www.ode.state.oh.us/reportcardfiles/2004–2005/BUILD/034900.pdf

Ohio Department of Education. (2006). *Canton City School District: 2005–2006 school year report card.* Retrieved August 6, 2007, from http://www.ode.state.oh.us/reportcardfiles/2005–2006/DIST/043711.pdf

Rodriguez, M. C. (2004). The role of classroom assessment in student performance in TIMSS. *Applied Measurement in Education, 17*(1), 1–24.

Singleton, G. E., & Linton, C. (2006). *Courageous conversations about race: A field guide for achieving equity in schools.* Thousand Oaks, CA: Corwin Press.

Stiggins, R. J., Arter, J. A., Chappuis, J., & Chappuis, S. (2004). *Classroom assessment for student learning: Doing it right—Using it well.* Portland, OR: Assessment Training Institute.

Tennessee Department of Education. (2006). *Johnson County report card 2006.* Retrieved October 1, 2007, from http: //www.k-12.state.tn.us/rptcrd06/system2.asp?S=460

Zuman, J. (2006). *Using Data Project: Final evaluation report.* Unpublished report. Arlington, MA: Intercultural Center for Research in Education.

2 Getting Organized for Collaborative Inquiry

By Nancy Love

As you begin to consider using collaborative inquiry in your own setting, you may wonder: "Where can I start?" There are several key questions districts and schools consider as they lay the groundwork for successful implementation of collaborative inquiry. How can collaborative inquiry be integrated into existing improvement efforts and with other initiatives? How do you build support among key people? Organize Data Teams? Select and prepare Data Coaches? Create time for collaboration? Ensure timely access to robust local data? As Using Data schools and districts learned, the answers to these fundamental questions create the conditions that can make or break the success of collaborative inquiry.

In this chapter, we will look at six steps district and school leaders take to establish collaborative inquiry within their schools. We will focus most intensively on Steps 3 and 4, looking closely at the critical role Data Coaches and Data Teams play in implementing collaborative inquiry.

Based on material from *The Data Coach's Guide to Improving Learning for All Students: Unleashing the Power of Collaborative Inquiry* (2008) by Nancy Love, Katherine E. Stiles, Susan Mundry, and Kathryn DiRanna. Adapted with permission from Corwin Press.

1. MAKE COLLABORATIVE INQUIRY AN INTEGRAL PART OF THE SCHOOL OPERATION AND IMPROVEMENT INITIATIVES

Often teachers and administrators are engaged in a variety of new programs and activities. Too often, these initiatives are disconnected and incoherent. To remedy this, district and school leaders integrate collaborative inquiry into school staff's ongoing work rather than treating it as an add-on. They know that the collaborative use of data is the foundation for any successful school improvement effort. "If you don't look at the data, everything else is just a guess," explained Mike Bayer, principal investigator of the Stark County Math and Science Partnership and Using Data Project collaborator from Stark County, Ohio. "The data give us direction on where to focus to raise achievement."

As you prepare for collaborative inquiry, consider to what extent data are now embedded in your existing school operation. What happens now when teachers get student-learning data? Does the district's data management system suggest ways to use data to enhance results? Do grade-level teams look at student results together? The collaborative inquiry process of examining data can be applied in any of these contexts. Are you engaged in school improvement initiatives such as implementing new curricula, technology, or professional learning communities? If so, using data in an ongoing way will help ensure that your improvement initiatives are focused on the areas that are most critical for improving student learning and will help you measure your progress and results.

Before implementing collaborative inquiry, district and school leaders consider their school's procedures related to data use as well as all the school improvement initiatives currently under way within the school or district. They talk to the people involved with data use and explore ideas for linking collaborative inquiry with current school procedures. They also think about how the existing initiatives might support each other and share rather than compete for resources, including staff time, energy, and commitment. They coordinate with leaders of other initiatives to develop a plan for communicating with them about their actions and progress. Coordination is especially important with other data initiatives, such as the implementation of data management systems.

For example, the Clark County School District in Las Vegas, Nevada, instituted a systemwide data management system a year after fifteen of their schools began to implement collaborative inquiry. Some participants saw the two initiatives as competing, while others saw the new data management system as replacing collaborative inquiry. Other schools, however, understood that the two initiatives could be complementary. The data management system provided the timely access to data, and the Using Data Process of Collaborative Inquiry gave teachers the tools to put those data to work to improve their instruction. The schools that were clear about the synergy between the two initiatives were able to adapt both to better meet the needs of their students (Zuman, 2006).

2. BUILD STAKEHOLDER SUPPORT

The success or failure of collaborative inquiry rests on the commitment and support of key stakeholders. Karen Brighton, project director of a systemic reform initiative in Arizona, put it this way:

> Stakeholder support is foundational. This is serious work and requires serious conversations. We went to the people in the districts and had multiple conversations. We went to the school boards. When the superintendents changed, we went back and retraced our steps. You need to stay the course to build real commitment, not just a signature.

Table 2.1 lists the audiences involved in launching this work and provides suggestions for how to work with them to build interest and

Table 2.1   Building Stakeholder Support

Audience	How to Engage	Their Role in Sustaining Collaborative Inquiry
District administrators	Meet with district administrators to provide an overview and share results other districts have had with collaborative inquiry; ask for their support and provide examples of the specific ways they can help.	Communicate your vision clearly and often. Require alignment of curricula, standards, and assessments. Commit to developing Data Coaches and Data Teams. Provide professional development to support collaborative inquiry. Require participation of principals. Create a safe environment for data use. Provide teachers with timely access to data and time to meet. Support the development and use of common benchmark assessments.
School administrators	Meet with building administrators to review the goals and process for collaborative inquiry and plan how to communicate with the entire school community.	Communicate your vision clearly and often. Be a strong supporter of the Data Team and of data use. Create a safe environment for data use. Actively participate as a member of a Data Team. Delegate Data Team leadership to a Data Coach. Empower teachers to make instructional decisions based on data. Help the team access resources, e.g., research or curriculum materials. Model the practice of using data. Provide teachers with timely access to data and time to meet.
School faculty	Lead a presentation on collaborative inquiry for all faculty; plan to give regular updates on the Data Team's work to all faculty.	Actively participate on Data Teams or sessions led by Data Teams. Use data to improve teaching. Keep informed of Data Team's work if not on a team. Take collective responsibility for improving student learning.
Department chairs, opinion leaders, union representatives, instructional coaches, and specialists	Check in with key people to see if they need more information about the process and to address any concerns.	Be a strong supporter of the Data Team and of data use. Actively participate as a member of a Data Team. Provide guidance and resources for Data Teams. Model using data in your own practice.

Audience	How to Engage	Their Role in Sustaining Collaborative Inquiry
		Provide teachers with timely access to data and time to meet. Advocate for collaborative inquiry among faculty.
Potential Data Team members	Conduct an informational meeting and/or one-on-one conversations about what is entailed in serving as a Data Team member and the benefits.	See the list in Step 4, "Organize Data Teams," later in this chapter.
School board members	Conduct a short presentation at a board meeting to explain what you are doing and why.	Support policies that provide time and resources for Data Coaches and Data Teams.
School improvement team	Attend school improvement team meetings to discuss how collaborative inquiry can support that team's work.	Coordinate efforts with Data Teams. Model the practice of using data to inform school improvement decisions.
Parents	Introduce parents to collaborative inquiry, including data on results, through the newsletter or listserv; provide overview at parents' night or PTO meeting.	Keep informed of Data Teams' work. Participate in Data Team–sponsored events for parents. Respond promptly to requests for data, such as parent surveys.
Data or assessment coordinators	Meet with the staff responsible for assessment and data to inform them of your plans and to learn how to work together to access district data.	Provide systems for timely access to local data. Stay in communication with Data Coach.

SOURCE: From *The Data Coach's Guide to Improving Learning for All Students: Unleashing the Power of Collaborative Inquiry* (pp. 31–32), by N. Love, K. E. Stiles, S. Mundry, and K. DiRanna, 2008, Thousand Oaks, CA: Corwin Press. Reprinted with permission.

engagement. The third column describes each audience's role in sustaining collaborative inquiry. Ultimately, the program's success hinges on each of these stakeholders helping to create a system within the district that supports continuous improvement. District and school leaders can use this table to guide their conversations with stakeholders, make requests, and as the basis for cooperative agreements that each stakeholder signs. The following vignette illustrates how one district leader went about building stakeholder support for collaborative inquiry.

Building Stakeholder Support at the District and Building Level

In Clark County, Nevada, the coordinator of K–5 Mathematics and Science, Thelma Davis, built stakeholder support for implementing collaborative inquiry in a variety of ways. She showed district leaders how using collaborative inquiry was closely aligned with the district's goals to increase data use, improve student achievement, and meet accountability requirements. She communicated with leaders of the Mathematics and Science Enhancement (MASE) Project, an ongoing initiative funded by the National Science Foundation that focused on implementing inquiry-based approaches to teaching and learning in collaborative settings. She explained how this collaborative approach to using data actually furthered the work of the project and made sure that MASE schools were included among participants. She met with regional superintendents and codeveloped an implementation plan with them. The plan included three participating schools in each of the district's regions, helping to build the regional superintendent's support, and also required that principals, as well as teacher–leaders, participate fully in training and implementation. Finally, she recognized that keeping stakeholders committed to the project required ongoing communication. She invited key district and building leaders to events and stayed in regular communication with them about the project and its progress.

As indicated in Table 2.1, there are several strategies suggested for different audiences to build their understanding of collaborative inquiry. Think carefully about who needs to be involved in local sites, how much time they can be involved, and make choices accordingly. As district and school leaders build stakeholder support, they keep the following outcomes in mind:

- All key stakeholders understand what collaborative inquiry is and how it will be used to enhance student learning.
- There is a process in place for ongoing communication about the project.
- There is a list of people who may be interested in serving on the Data Team(s).
- The building principal and/or a key administrator such as a curriculum coordinator or department chair agree to be actively involved in the process.
- The assessment or data coordinator understands the project and is lined up to assist with access to data.

3. SELECT, PREPARE, AND EMPOWER DATA COACHES

Chances are there is no one at your school or the schools you work with right now who is officially known as a Data Coach. This is a new role that is emerging as schools become more focused on using their data effectively to improve results. One of the most important findings from the four years of implementing the Using Data Project in schools across the country is that Data Coaches are the linchpin of successful collaborative inquiry. Without them, participating schools would not

> *Effective [Data Coaches] are key to the long-term sustainability of the Using Data Process.*
>
> —John Zuman (2006, p. 12)

have achieved the gains they realized in student learning, increased collaboration and data use, instructional improvement, or school culture.

Data Coach: An educational leader who guides Data Teams through the process of collaborative inquiry and influences the culture of schools to be one in which data are used continuously, collaboratively, and effectively to improve teaching and learning.

The Data Coach Role

You may have a clear picture in your minds of different kinds of coaches, such as instructional coaches or sports coaches. But what does a Data Coach do? In collaborative inquiry, the Data Coach plays three major roles, as illustrated in Figure 2.1.

> *If you want to take control and make it run your way, just do it yourself. If you want to build a team, you have to let that team evolve—with some parameters. Make it clear that we are not going to complain about kids or make excuses. The only thing we can work on is what we have control over.*
>
> —Ann Wacker, mathematics and Data Coach, Plain Local Schools, Canton, Ohio

Model and Spread Data Literacy. In the inner circle, the Data Coach's central role is modeling and spreading data literacy among all of the Data Team. *Data literacy* is the ability to interpret and use multiple data sources effectively to improve teaching and learning. Data Coaches are instrumental in gathering data for Data Teams, but they do not do the data analysis themselves. They lead the Data Team through the process of digging into the data to see what can be learned from it. Like a football or soccer coach, they are often on the sidelines while the Data Team is in the game, making their own sense of the data and using it to improve performance. But the Data Coach makes sure that the team has the resources—the data, the skills, the tools, and the practice—to do its job well.

Figure 2.1 The Data Coach Role

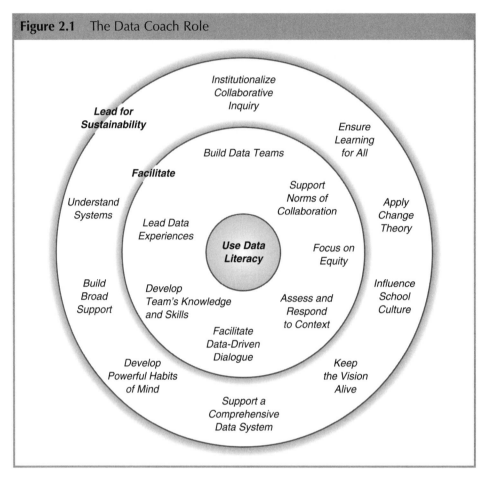

SOURCE: From *The Data Coach's Guide to Improving Learning for All Students: Unleashing the Power of Collaborative Inquiry* (p. 36), by N. Love, K. E. Stiles, S. Mundry, and K. DiRanna, 2008, Thousand Oaks, CA: Corwin Press. Reprinted with permission.

Facilitate the Data Team. The next ring in the circle illustrates the Data Coach's role as *facilitator.* Data Coaches convene the Data Teams, plan team meetings, facilitate dialogue, and guide the team through collaborative inquiry. While Data Coaches play the role of facilitator, they are not always neutral. They take a stand for promoting equity and effective learning for all students. They speak their truth and challenge assumptions and practices that get in the way of providing all students with a high-quality education. At the same time, they create an environment where each team member feels safe saying what he or she thinks.

As facilitator, the Data Coach will do the following:

- Build Data Teams: create high-functioning teams that talk about difficult issues and take effective action together
- Support norms of collaboration: guide teams to commit to, apply, and become skilled at group norms

- Focus on equity: take a stand for all students against racism and other forms of bias and encourage the team to do the same
- Assess and respond to context: use data about the team, students, and school to tailor collaborative inquiry to local realities, shifting as the context shifts
- Facilitate Data-Driven Dialogue: help the team separate observation from inference and examine assumptions
- Develop team's knowledge and skills: develop team members' knowledge and skills for high-capacity data use (uses that lead to improved teaching and learning), including the following:

  o Data literacy and collaborative inquiry knowledge and skills: build the capacity of others to engage with data productively
  o Content knowledge, generic pedagogical knowledge, and pedagogical content knowledge: keep the focus on improving instruction; guide the team to deepen their own knowledge of content, pedagogy, and pedagogical content as they analyze data and implement solutions
  o Cultural proficiency: encourage the team to better understand and interact respectfully with diverse cultures and respond to data in respectful ways
  o Leadership and facilitation skills: develop others' leadership and facilitation skills; grow more Data Coaches!

- Lead data experiences: lead Data Teams through the process of collaborative inquiry

Provide Leadership for Sustainability. The third major area of responsibility for Data Coaches is to provide *leadership for sustainability* of the practice of collaborative inquiry to continuously enhance student learning. Specifically, Data Coaches do the following:

- Institutionalize collaborative inquiry: pay attention to what it takes to sustain the use of collaborative inquiry, including involving key people and leaders; building the culture to support the practice; working to infuse collaborative inquiry into ongoing structures such as faculty meetings, curriculum and other committees, and policy decisions; and making the use of student data to inform action and expectation for all staff
- Ensure learning for all: use their influence to convince people of the importance of intervening when data show low levels of learning for any students and to shift conversations away from blame and toward collective responsibility for closing achievement gaps
- Apply change theory: understand that their role is to build awareness and support among all key players in the schools and districts,

to provide ample opportunities for people to clarify what collaborative inquiry is and why it is beneficial for the school, to help as many staff as possible to develop data literacy skills, to encourage administrators to sanction the use of collaborative inquiry, and to provide structures such as time to support its use

- Influence school culture: model the cultural shifts needed, such as use of data, dialogue, and collaboration, and engage Data Teams and other key stakeholders in building a vision of the culture they want to create for their school

- Keep the vision alive: look for opportunities to celebrate successes, supporting the Data Team, administrators, and other key stakeholders to share their success stories and document how collaborative inquiry is helping to solve student-learning problems

- Support a comprehensive data system: work with the Data Team, administrators, and others to support the school and district to use a comprehensive data system that provides timely and accurate information on student learning and other important outcomes

- Develop powerful habits of mind: lead by example to build a shared vision for collaborative inquiry in the school and walk the talk by demonstrating powerful habits of mind (see Table 2.2), such as shifting conversations from resignation, complaints, and resistance to possibility by using subtle language shifts—"I can" and "I will" instead of "I should" and "I must" (Ellis, 2002; Sparks, 2007)

- Build broad support: meet with central office administrators to explain what collaborative inquiry is and why it is an essential tool for the district (understanding that school improvement happens in the broader context of the school district), regularly update key administrators on what is being accomplished and what has to happen next, and make presentations at parent and teacher meetings to raise awareness of the use of collaborative inquiry

- Understand systems: build on all of the actions listed above, understand that the school and district operate as a system that is also part of a broader community and state system, think about how to leverage state policies such as requirements for data reporting and student achievement to encourage the school to build a culture for data use and ongoing improvement, know their context well and think strategically about how to build on strengths and diminish weaknesses

Criteria for Selecting Data Coaches

Few people come with the full complement of knowledge and skills that are desirable for Data Coaches. Data Coaches are made, not born.

Table 2.2 Habits of Mind Shifts

From	To
Resignation, complaints, and resistance	Possibility, self-determination, and commitment
Unclear values, purpose, and goals	Clear, focused goals, clarified purpose and values
Single conversation	Sustained, persistent interaction
Unclear points of view	Clear, succinct, data-driven, powerfully expressed points of view
Superficial attending	Committed listening
Your truth as the truth	Reliance on data to support conclusions

SOURCE: Adapted from *Leading for Results* (2nd ed.), by D. Sparks, 2007, Thousand Oaks, CA: Corwin Press. Reprinted with permission.

NOTE: This table is also used in *The Data Coach's Guide to Improving Learning for All Students: Unleashing the Power of Collaborative Inquiry* (p. 38), by N. Love, K. E. Stiles, S. Mundry, and K. DiRanna, 2008, Thousand Oaks, CA: Corwin Press.

They will develop over time through training and experience. In selecting Data Coaches, district and school leaders consider the following criteria:

- They look for someone with the sanction or authority of the district or school administration. Data Coaches can operate only if their role is officially sanctioned and they have the authority, time, and legitimacy to convene and lead Data Teams. Often, instructional, assessment, or school improvement coaches or coordinators; principals or assistant principals; or team leaders become Data Coaches.

> *Interpersonal communication is key. If you develop a relationship with people, they will work with you. You've also got to be very comfortable with the data.*
>
> —Ann Wacker, mathematics and Data Coach, Plain Local Schools, Canton, Ohio

- They look for demonstrated leadership in instructional improvement, either as an effective and collaborative teacher, an instructional coach, or an administrator who garners the respect of others and is an instructional leader.
- They look for moral commitment to ensuring equity and learning for all students. The role of Data Coach calls for someone who is

passionate about equity, willing to stand up for their beliefs, and committed to strengthening their own cultural proficiency.

- They look for skill as a collaborator and team facilitator.
- They look for basic knowledge of school data and assessments. Data Coaches do not need to be experts in statistics or complex data management systems, but they should know the basics of interpreting results and not be afraid of data. Basic knowledge of Excel is a plus.
- They look for willingness to take risks, make mistakes, and continuously learn.

Developing Data Coaches

A key learning from the Using Data Project is that Data Coaches require in-depth professional development keyed to their specialized role in spreading data literacy, facilitating Data Teams, and sustaining ongoing collaborative inquiry. Like any good professional development, professional learning for Data Coaches is most effective when the following elements are present (Loucks-Horsley, Love, Stiles, Mundry, & Hewson, 2003):

We learn by doing—if we reflect on what we do.

—John Dewey

- Opportunities for in-depth learning of the specific knowledge and skills they will use as Data Coaches. These opportunities include data literacy and collaborative inquiry knowledge and skills; content knowledge, generic pedagogical knowledge, and pedagogical content knowledge; cultural proficiency; and leadership and facilitation skills. Professional development strategies for learning this knowledge base can include a wide range of experiences, such as workshops or study groups, as well as opportunities to apply this knowledge with practice and coaching. The Using Data Project engaged Data Coaches in learning and applying this knowledge base over a three-year period. The project also collaborated with ongoing mathematics and science improvement projects that were focused on developing teachers' content knowledge and pedagogical content knowledge.
- Learning experiences based on research about adult and student learning. For example, workshops provided by the Using Data Project
  - were staged over a period of one and a half years, with time in between for Data Coaches to practice what they were learning with actual Data Teams then come back together to debrief their experiences and learn new content;
  - provided opportunities for Data Coaches to experience as learners the same activities and tools they would then lead for Data Teams;
  - started with and built on Data Coaches' prior knowledge and skill;

- included ample time for in-depth investigations, collaborative work, and reflection;
- connected explicitly to Data Coaches' real work with data and Data Teams, using both their own and simulated data and reflecting on how activities would apply to their context;
- used practical, hands-on materials to guide implementation (now available in *The Data Coach's Guide to Improving Learning for All Students: Unleashing the Power of Collaborative Inquiry;* Love, Stiles, Mundry, & DiRanna, 2008).

- **Opportunities to practice with feedback and support.** Like teachers, Data Coaches learn on the job, in this case by actually leading collaborative inquiry with Data Teams. But without support they can easily get discouraged and derailed. It is important that Data Coaches have the opportunity to reflect on their experiences both with their peers and with experts. The Using Data Project provided three years of ongoing support to Data Coaches, which included

  - observing Data Coaches with Data Teams and providing them with feedback;
  - convening Data Coaches for problem solving and troubleshooting meetings;
  - training Super Data Coaches at the district level, who were on call to support school-based Data Coaches and teams;
  - intervening with principals and district and project leaders to rally their support for the Data Coaches.

Allocating Time for Data Coaches

Data Coaches need protected time to play their role in school improvement. How much time? Some Data Coaches in the Using Data Project worked full-time leading Data Teams in just one school. This was their job. These Data Coaches gathered and prepared common assessment data and facilitated the process for all the grade-level teams in every content area in their buildings. In most of the elementary and middle schools in Clark County, Nevada, three Data Coaches (a principal and two full-time teachers) shared the role. In Canton City, Ohio, two full-time Data Coaches, one focused on mathematics and one on science, served four middle schools, while two more full-time Data Coaches, again with one focused on mathematics and one on science, served the district's two major high schools.

4. ORGANIZE DATA TEAMS

After selecting a Data Coach, district and school leaders consider whom to invite to join the Data Team. They keep the purpose of the Data Team in mind and use that as a criterion for membership.

Data Team: A team of four to eight teachers, other school faculty, and ideally their building administrator who work together to use data to improve student learning.

Data Teams can take many different forms. For example, if the purpose is to use collaborative inquiry in a particular subject area such as language arts or mathematics, the team should include teachers and other staff who have responsibilities in this area, such as members of the district's curriculum committee and staff who have been involved in other related initiatives (e.g., textbook selection and professional development planning in these subjects). If the purpose is to use collaborative inquiry to look across all subject areas, the team should be balanced to include members from across the different curriculum areas. Other equally important considerations are racial/ethnic diversity and inclusion of specialists such as teachers of English language learners or of students with exceptional needs.

At an elementary school, Data Teams are often composed of representatives of different grade levels and focused on a particular content area, such as mathematics. Or they can be a school improvement team or leadership team looking at all content areas and grade levels. In some elementary schools, there is a schoolwide Data Team with representatives from each grade level, who in turn lead grade-level Data Teams.

In a middle school, junior high, or high school, Data Teams are generally organized by department or content area. In some cases, all the members of the department comprise the Data Team. In others, the Data Team is a smaller representative group from the department. In high schools, teachers who teach the same course may form a Data Team. In schools organized as professional learning communities with all teachers participating in teams, those teams function as Data Teams. In the Using Data Project, many schools started out with just one Data Team but later expanded to include every teacher as a member of a Data Team.

There may be a group already in place that district and school leaders can tap for the Data Team. For example, schools may have a group of teacher-leaders who are responsible for mentoring other teachers or a school improvement committee. Look for people who are opinion leaders, reflect different perspectives, and can be ambassadors to others for the project. While membership on Data Teams is usually on a volunteer basis, district and school leaders may encourage people who might not volunteer right away to consider being a part of the team. Relying on the "usual suspects" who volunteer for everything can sometimes result in a team of people with too many competing demands on their time and/or who are not representative of the diversity in your school. District and school leaders may want to consider tapping individuals who are even somewhat skeptical of the process. These individuals can be particularly helpful in identifying roadblocks and concerns that others may be thinking but are not comfortable voicing.

What Do Data Teams Do?

Data Teams engage in collaborative inquiry, using a variety of types of data to inquire into how to improve teaching and learning. Typical responsibilities for Data Team members include the following:

- Collecting and analyzing a variety of types of school data
- Developing or adapting common assessment instruments
- Committing to norms of collaboration and to examining data from an equity perspective
- Identifying student-learning problems, verifying causes, generating solutions, and monitoring and achieving results for students
- Consulting research to investigate problems, causes, and best practice
- Developing data-supported action plans
- Communicating with staff and key stakeholders about the findings and the plans
- Overseeing the implementation of the plan (schoolwide or vertical team) and/or implementing instructional improvement in their own classrooms (grade-level, course, or subject teams)
- Sharing successes and challenges from their own classrooms and/or at the school level
- Engaging a broader group of stakeholders to gain their input, involvement, and commitment
- Coordinating with other school or district initiatives and leaders
- Developing their data literacy and collaborative inquiry knowledge and skills; content knowledge, generic pedagogical knowledge, and pedagogical content knowledge; cultural proficiency; and leadership and facilitation skills

Clarifying Roles and Responsibilities

With new structures such as Data Teams and new roles such as Data Coaches, it is important to clarify roles and responsibilities. As district and school leaders plan to launch Data Teams, they meet with district and building administrators to clarify the role of the team and its decision-making authority. For example, can the team decide to implement interventions to address student-learning problems or are they responsible for recommendations to someone else for that decision? What ongoing feedback should be provided and to whom about the Data Team's findings? What

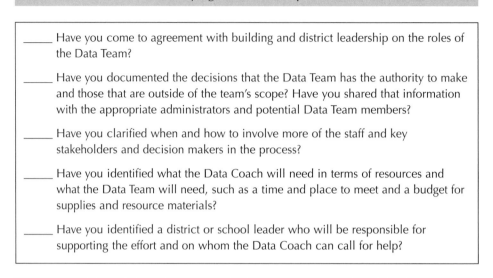

Table 2.3   Checklist for Clarifying Roles and Responsibilities

_____ Have you come to agreement with building and district leadership on the roles of the Data Team?

_____ Have you documented the decisions that the Data Team has the authority to make and those that are outside of the team's scope? Have you shared that information with the appropriate administrators and potential Data Team members?

_____ Have you clarified when and how to involve more of the staff and key stakeholders and decision makers in the process?

_____ Have you identified what the Data Coach will need in terms of resources and what the Data Team will need, such as a time and place to meet and a budget for supplies and resource materials?

_____ Have you identified a district or school leader who will be responsible for supporting the effort and on whom the Data Coach can call for help?

SOURCE: From *The Data Coach's Guide to Improving Learning for All Students: Unleashing the Power of Collaborative Inquiry* (p. 42), by N. Love, K. E. Stiles, S. Mundry, and K. DiRanna, 2008, Thousand Oaks, CA: Corwin Press. Reprinted with permission.

resources are needed and how will they be provided? The checklist of roles and responsibilities in Table 2.3 can guide district and school leaders as they clarify roles and responsibilities of their Data Teams.

5. ESTABLISH TIME FOR COLLABORATION

Teaching is a three-part act—planning, doing, and reflecting. Unfortunately, school schedules are often based on the assumption that if teachers are not in the classroom in front of students, they are not doing their job. The school day typically has provided time for teaching, but not for the equally important functions of planning and reflecting. Stigler and Hiebert (1999) create an image of a teacher's day that is not unlike a college professor's, with time for teaching and research, collaborative planning and reflecting with colleagues, and "office hours" with individual students. While this vision may not become a reality in schools in the near future, changing the school schedule somewhat to create time for teacher collaboration is a requirement for collaborative inquiry. A growing body of research linking teacher collaboration with student achievement makes this conclusion inescapable and urgent: time for teacher collaboration is not a luxury (Little, 1990; Louis, Kruse, & Marks, 1996; McLaughlin & Talbert, 2001). It is a necessity for schools that want to improve.

How much time? Along with many school improvement experts, we recommend a minimum of forty-five minutes per week of uninterrupted, protected time for collaboration. Many schools participating in the Using Data Project were able to carve out weekly or even daily time for teachers to work together by creative use of specialists, block scheduling, or reallocation of teacher contract time. Others convened the Data Team quarterly for a full release-day of analyzing common benchmark assessment results along with two- to three-day data retreats in the summer. The growing number of schools across the country that now schedule time for teacher collaboration during the school day proves that finding time is a solvable problem when the will is present to do so.

Finding Time for Data Teams

- Buy time

  - Hire substitutes
  - Provide summer stipends

- Make time

  - Modify the school schedule to ten minutes earlier each day, banking time for collaboration
  - Start school late or end early one day per week
  - Use common planning time

- Rethink time

  - Use special teachers to cover classrooms
  - Release teams of teachers from lunch or recess duty and use the extra time for collaboration
  - Review funding sources (e.g., use Title I funds to hire part-time teachers)
  - Use common time such as grade-level meetings or daily common planning time
  - Regroup students (e.g., have three classes covered by two specialists)
  - Use one prep period per week

- Use existing time more effectively (e.g., faculty or grade-level meetings)

SOURCES: Dempsey, 2007; Johnston, Knight, and Miller, 2007; Khorsheed, 2007.

6. ENSURE TIMELY ACCESS TO ROBUST LOCAL DATA SOURCES

In the early days of the Using Data Project, staff confronted a confounding obstacle: The very people who could make the best use of student-learning data—the teachers—had the least access to the data. Test data were "under lock and key" and were the "private property" of the research, assessment, or other district office. Teachers often did not receive assessment data at all or received them so long after the tests were administered that they were not even teaching the same children. Project staff and district- and school-based collaborators had to advocate strongly to democratize the data, giving teachers access to their students' results. Thankfully, times are changing as more districts put timely data systems into place that make a variety of school data readily available to teachers.

> By the end of the 2004–2005 school year, most grade levels had given some common assessments and had tried to compile the data. We did this using Math–Science Partnership project time during the school day. This was a long process because we had to compile the data by hand. We had no time left to actually dive into it and discover what we needed to change in terms of instructional strategies. All that changed with the purchase of the Principia software package. Now we are able to use that same time to make data-driven decisions.
>
> —Ann Wacker, mathematics and Data Coach, Plain Local Schools, Canton, Ohio

Even with the best data management systems, however, data access can still be problematic. For example, many states do not report data at the item level or release test items for teachers to analyze. Yet item-level data, when used in conjunction with the actual test items, are among the most useful data teachers have to improve their instruction.

One way around this problem is for schools to make or buy their own assessments and ensure that teachers have just-in-time access to both the item-level results and the items themselves. This is one reason why common benchmark assessments are so important to instructional improvement. Because they lend themselves to item analysis, are administered periodically throughout the school year, and align with local standards and curricula, they can fuel collaborative inquiry.

Another challenge is to get results from common assessments to teachers quickly, within a few days—in time for them to actually *do* something with those results. Fortunately, this problem has a simple technological solution: inexpensive software programs and scanners, which can scan about 200 tests per hour, placed within easy access of the Data Coach. When put in place in participating Using Data Project schools, these machines removed the data bottleneck and got collaborative inquiry moving.

The good news is that much of the data that fuels collaborative inquiry is not dependent on expensive data management systems. Simple scanners will do the job of churning out the item-level data on local assessments. Some of the most robust data sources, formative classroom assessments and common assessments such as student work, mathematics problems of the week, and science journals, require no data management system at all— just teachers collecting their students' work and sharing it with colleagues. While data management systems facilitate data access, they are not a prerequisite for collaborative inquiry.

SUMMARY

As you lay the groundwork for implementing collaborative inquiry in a school, district, or educational improvement project, keep in mind the adage "Go slow to go fast." It is well worth the time to create the conditions for success: (1) an effort that is aligned and integrated with other initiatives and data management; (2) buy-in from key stakeholders; (3) well-prepared Data Coaches with the authority and time to carry out their role; (4) Data Teams of teachers and administrators established at the school, grade level, department, and/or course level; (5) a minimum of forty-five minutes weekly for Data Teams to work together; and (6) the mechanisms for giving teachers timely access (within days of the assessment) to student-learning data, especially at the item level.

REFERENCES

Dempsey, N. (2007). Five elements combine in a formula for coaching. *Journal of Staff Development, 28*(2), 10–13.

Ellis, D. (2002). *Falling awake: Creating the life of your dreams.* Rapid City, SD: Breakthrough Enterprises.

Johnston, J., Knight, M., & Miller, L. (2007). Finding time for teams. *Journal of Staff Development, 28*(2), 14–18.

Khorsheed, K. (2007). Four places to dig deep to find more time for teacher collaboration. *Journal of Staff Development, 28*(2), 43–45.

Little, J. W. (1990). Teachers as colleagues. In A. Lieberman (Ed.), *Schools as collaborative cultures: Creating the future now* (pp. 165–193). New York: Palmer.

Loucks-Horsley, S., Love, N., Stiles, K. E., Mundry, S., & Hewson, P. W. (2003). *Designing professional development for teachers of science and mathematics* (2nd ed.). Thousand Oaks, CA: Corwin Press.

Louis, K. S., Kruse, S., & Marks, H. (1996). Schoolwide professional community. In F. Newmann and Associates (Eds.), *Authentic achievement: Restructuring schools for intellectual quality* (pp. 179–203). San Francisco: Jossey-Bass.

Love, N., Stiles, K. E., Mundry, S., & DiRanna, K. (2008). *The data coach's guide to improving learning for all students: Unleashing the power of collaborative inquiry.* Thousand Oaks, CA: Corwin Press.

McLaughlin, M. W., & Talbert, J. (2001). *Professional communities and the work of high school teaching.* Chicago: University of Chicago Press.

Sparks, D. (2007). *Leading for results* (2nd ed.). Thousand Oaks, CA: Corwin Press.

Stigler, J. W., & Hiebert, J. (1999). *The teaching gap: Best ideas from the world's teachers for improving education in the classroom.* New York: Free Press.

Zuman, J. (2006). *Using Data Project: Final evaluation report.* Unpublished report. Arlington, MA: Intercultural Center for Research in Education.

3 The Using Data Process

A Model for Collaborative Inquiry

By Nancy Love

J ust like inquiry-based instruction in the classroom, collaborative inquiry works best when teachers have a model to follow—a sequence of steps that guides the inquiry and helps ensure productive dialogue and results. It is one thing to say "go forward and collaborate" and hope for the best. We have all suffered in teams that flounder with lack of direction or simply recreate old patterns of thinking and responding. It is far more effective to equip Data Teams and Data Coaches with a process that structures their work together and helps them avoid the many possible pitfalls of continuous improvement, such as the following:

- Lack of a moral compass to ground the work in a commitment to equity and to learning for all students
- Use of single and imperfect measures as the basis for decision making
- Blaming students and their backgrounds for achievement gaps
- Making assumptions about causes of student-learning problems without using research and local data to verify them

Based on material from *The Data Coach's Guide to Improving Learning for All Students: Unleashing the Power of Collaborative Inquiry* (2008) by Nancy Love, Katherine E. Stiles, Susan Mundry, and Kathryn DiRanna. Adapted with permission from Corwin Press.

- Failure to carefully think through action plans to logically link actions to results
- Unclear or overambitious goals
- Little or no monitoring of implementation or results

This chapter describes the Using Data Process of Collaborative Inquiry (the Using Data Process for short), one model for collaborative inquiry that has been carefully crafted to avoid these pitfalls. It elaborates on each of the process's five stages, including its rationale, sample tools, and real-life examples. This chapter also teases out essential features that have accounted for the success of the Using Data Process and can be applied to any approach to continuous improvement. Our purpose is to raise awareness about one successful approach while guiding readers to be critical consumers of improvement processes. For a comprehensive implementation guide to the Using Data Process, including tools, processes, and background information and notes for Data Coaches, see *The Data Coach's Guide to Improving Learning for All Students: Unleashing the Power of Collaborative Inquiry* by Nancy Love, Katherine E. Stiles, Susan Mundry, and Kathryn DiRanna (2008). See also Chapter 6 for a case study of a Data Team implementing the Using Data Process.

A Flexible Structure for Collaborative Inquiry

While there are many models for continuous improvement, the Using Data Process, illustrated in Figure 3.1, is one that has been used successfully in collaboration with mathematics and science improvement initiatives across the country, including in Canton, Ohio, Las Vegas, Nevada, and rural Arizona and Tennessee. Schools implementing the Using Data Process produced the following results (for more on results, see Chapter 1):

- Narrowed the achievement gaps between students with exceptional needs and general education students in all content areas and grade levels
- Increased the percentage of African American students proficient in high school mathematics by 74%
- Demonstrated significant and steady gains in mathematics in elementary, middle, and high schools
- Cut the failure rate of Native American children in half
- Increased collaboration and reflection on practice among teachers
- Increased teachers' engagement in frequent and in-depth use of multiple data sources, including high-stakes, formative, and benchmark assessments as well as data about practice
- Made instructional improvements based on data analysis (Zuman, 2006)

Figure 3.1   The Using Data Process of Collaborative Inquiry

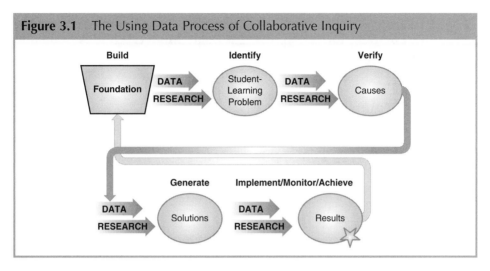

SOURCE: From *The Data Coach's Guide to Improving Learning for All Students: Unleashing the Power of Collaborative Inquiry* (p. 21), by N. Love, K. E. Stiles, S. Mundry, and K. DiRanna, 2008, Thousand Oaks, CA: Corwin Press. Reprinted with permission.

When Using Data Project staff began their work with these schools, they did not have a fleshed-out model for Data Coaches to follow. Soon the Data Coaches were clamoring for one. "How do we get started?" "When do we do what?" "What do we do if the team starts blaming students?" Staff quickly set to work to provide a process that was both structured and adaptable to local conditions, which were very different in Las Vegas, for example, than they were in a small rural school on an Indian reservation. The results of these efforts are the Using Data Process, a road map for collaborative inquirers to follow that is easily adapted for different contexts. The model itself, in fact, calls for Data Teams to assess, understand, and respond to their own context, adjusting the process accordingly. An underlying principle of the model, then, is that it is a guide, not a prescription, to follow for continuous improvement.

The Using Data Process incorporates five stages, each of which is described in more detail in this chapter:

1. Building a solid foundation for collaborative inquiry by establishing shared values, vision, and parameters for Data Team work

2. Identifying a student-learning problem on which to focus improvement by analyzing multiple data sources

3. Verifying causes of the identified student-learning problem through use of research and local data about practice

4. Generating solutions by drawing on research and best practice and planning for action, using a Logic Model to link solutions to intended results

5. Implementing solutions, while frequently monitoring both implementation and results, and celebrating successes

1. BUILDING THE FOUNDATION

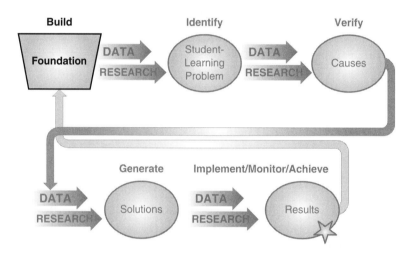

The first stage of the Using Data Process is Building the Foundation. In this part of the process, the Data Team builds a rock-solid foundation of commitments to each other, to all students' learning, and to the Using Data Process. These commitments help keep the Data Team standing strong and able to fulfill their larger purpose—improving teaching and learning and closing achievement gaps.

Like a strong building foundation, the work the team does in this part of the process helps them stand up to the pressures, conflicts, and challenges they will inevitably face. For example, when they begin their analysis of student-learning data, if comments reflect a lack of understanding and respect for African American students, the team will have language and tools for challenging those assumptions. If they grow discouraged by low test scores, they will have a compelling vision to keep them motivated. If conflict erupts in the group, they will have established collaborative norms to negotiate difficult conversations. Finally, decision-making authority and roles and responsibilities will be clearly established so there is no confusion about the team's authority to make decisions and take action.

> *What really attracted me to the Using Data Process were the foundational pieces—finding out what the context is, getting that commitment, asking "Do we want to go in the same direction? Build collaborative leadership? Have the same goals?" If I have one piece of advice for others, it is to do more about laying the groundwork.*
>
> —Karen Brighton, program manager, Arizona Rural Systemic Initiative

There are four important steps Data Teams take to build the foundation: (1) they launch Data Teams, (2) study the context of their school, (3) raise awareness of cultural proficiency, and (4) envision a detailed future for their school or for specific content areas they wish to focus on. The work the Data Team does in carrying out these four steps is pertinent to every subsequent stage in the Using Data Process. They establish the parameters, understandings, values, and vision that will guide the Data Team throughout.

Building the Foundation

- Launch Data Teams
- Study the school's context
- Raise awareness of cultural proficiency
- Envision a detailed future for the school or program

Launch Data Teams

To get started as a Data Team, the Data Coach and the new team work together to answer the following questions:

- What is the collaborative inquiry model we will be engaged with?
- What is our purpose as a team?
- What are our specific roles and responsibilities? What kinds of decisions will we be authorized to make? How will we interact with other initiatives and stakeholders?
- How will we work together? What collaborative norms will guide our team's work together? How will we create a safe environment to look at data, face the facts, and have difficult and candid conversations?

Study the School's Context

To understand their context, the Data Team studies demographic data to learn about the diversity of the students they serve, their community, and their faculty. They also assess the current state of their school culture and consider the changes in culture, equity, trust, instruction, data use, collaboration, leadership, and capacity that they will help bring about in their school as they move toward a high-performing data culture. This step builds the Data Team's foundation for responding to data based

> We are always working on norms of collaboration in our team of field staff and Data Coaches. We individually choose a norm to focus on, pair up to coach each other, and collect data to debrief. This has made a huge difference in including everyone's voice and embracing the diversity of our team, which includes Native Americans and Whites, males and females.
>
> —Karen Brighton, program manager, Arizona Rural System Initiative

on an understanding of who their students are. It also strengthens their ability to both operate effectively within their current culture while acting to strengthen it.

Raise Awareness of Cultural Proficiency

Effective collaborative inquiry puts equity—the right of all students to achieve at high levels—in the forefront and equips teachers with language and tools for dealing constructively with cultural diversity. This is hard but critically important work. Despite decades of educational reform, high-income, White, and Asian students continue to out-perform students living in poverty and African American, Latino/a, and Native American students on standardized tests, grades, class rank, and college-going rates (Johnson, 2002). Underlying these achievement differences is a long history of practices and beliefs that do harm to students who do not fit the mold of the dominant culture.

> *Blaming students for poor test scores is actually a part of the status quo. In this country, no matter what our color, we are all bombarded with information that is racist, classist, and sexist. Data Coaches have to spend significant time on building the foundation or we carry harmful ideas into the data dialogue with us. This became apparent during a training I conducted. A quarter of the participants missed the Building the Foundation stage of the program. The difference between the participants who experienced Building the Foundation and those that did not was huge. When we got into looking at the data, the participants without the foundational tasks did not have the same awareness about equity issues. They jumped to inferences about the limitations of certain students rather than questioning instructional practices. If you skip Building the Foundation you will put our children at risk. We have to attack harmful beliefs head on.*
>
> —Aminata Umoja,
> Using Data trainer and
> independent consultant, Atlanta, Georgia

Diversity is a reality in all schools. Even in predominantly affluent, White suburbs, there are some students who are not being served well. The question is not *if* Data Teams deal with diversity. The question is *how*. Examining data (especially demographic, achievement, and disaggregated data) frequently surfaces negative assumptions about what children of color, students with exceptional needs, or students living in poverty are capable of learning and achieving. Some team members may hold the view that the gaps are inevitable. Others might want to avoid talking about them either because they say they view all students as the same or because of shame about a group's performance. For many Data Team members, uncovering achievement gaps is shocking and upsetting. Data Teams can either sweep these issues under the rug or erupt in destructive conflict, or they can use data as a catalyst to examine and transform beliefs and practices that stand as barriers to student learning.

The key—and this is easier said than done—is acknowledging the realities of cultural differences, race and racism, and class and classism, and engaging in constructive dialogue about these issues throughout the process. The Using Data Project staff learned the hard way to provide concrete guidance to Data Coaches and teams about how to have these difficult conversations as they examine and react to data.

> **Cultural Proficiency:** "Honoring the differences among cultures, viewing diversity as a benefit, and interacting knowledgeably and respectfully among a variety of cultural groups" (Lindsey, Roberts, & CampbellJones, 2005, p. xviii).

In Building the Foundation, Data Teams study principles of cultural proficiency—deep knowledge and respect for diverse cultures—and the Cultural Proficiency Continuum, a framework for understanding a range of responses to diversity. These serve as a common language that helps Data Teams talk about diversity issues later as they dive into data analysis. From the beginning of the process, Data Teams consider how their assumptions about students and their capabilities will shape how they interpret and respond to data. These important conversations lay the foundation for using data as a catalyst to examining those assumptions, with the purpose of closing achievement gaps throughout the rest of the process.

Vignette

Using Data Staff Learn From Experience

While our program espoused a strong commitment to equity from the outset, we quickly learned that that was not enough. On the second day of our national field test, participants were engaged in dialogue about demographic data. Suddenly, and to our great surprise, conflict erupted in the group between a White and an African American participant. The staff was not equipped to handle it. At the same time, we realized that this kind of conflict is not unexpected, and, in fact, is likely when groups first start talking about race. We were missing an important opportunity if we did not prepare Data Coaches to handle these conversations productively. We were fortunate to have the help of four leading equity experts, who led us to strengthen the program. We added a focus on deepening Data Coaches' understanding of cultural proficiency and skill building in facilitating dialogue around issues of race/ethnicity, class, culture, gender, and other differences that inevitably arise from examining data. These themes of cultural proficiency are now incorporated throughout the program.

In addition, Data Coaches learn what to do when team members blame students and their circumstances for failure, choose causes that harm some students, or slip into cultural incompetence (e.g., "I just see kids as kids: I don't see color" or "Our kids from the other side of the tracks are never going to college. Why should they take this science course anyway?"). Data Coaches guide Data Teams to bring an "equity lens" to the data by considering interpretations and responses to data that reflect cultural competence and a commitment to equity. See Chapter 4 for more information on cultural proficiency, a critical theme in successful collaborative inquiry.

Strategies for Bringing an Equity Lens to Data

- Keep to the structure of Data-Driven Dialogue (introduced in the next section, Identifying a Student-Learning Problem).
- Be candid about your assumptions about students' ability to learn, and be open to dialogue about them.
- Periodically revisit the vision and values established in the Building the Foundation part of the process, asking to what extent your reactions to the data are consistent with that vision and those values.
- Use the Cultural Proficiency Continuum (see Chapter 4) to reflect on the inferences you are drawing from the data.
- Bring diverse voices to the Data Team, including students and parents. Use their perspectives to broaden your own.
- Disaggregate student learning and other data and make sure that data sources include diverse students' perspectives.
- Follow the verify-causes procedure described in this chapter rather than acting on your initial interpretations of the data.
- Keep the focus on instructional improvement and other causes of student-learning problems over which you have control.
- Make blaming students and their backgrounds off-limits.
- Commit to becoming a culturally proficient Data Team and school.

Envision a Detailed Future for the School or Program

The final step in Building the Foundation is for the Data Team to envision a detailed future for their school (or for a specific content area). Data Teams consider and clearly establish what they want students to know and be able to do; how they will assess to what extent students are learning that; how they will respond when students do not learn; what core values will guide them; and what they envision for curricula and instruction, equity, and critical supports such as professional development and school culture (see Figure 3.2). Answering these questions builds the foundation for Data Teams to use data to move toward this vision.

> How can you use data to drive instruction if you don't know what the instruction should be in the first place?
>
> —Pam Bernabei-Rorrer, mathematics and Data Coach, Canton City, Ohio

Figure 3.2 School of Our Dreams

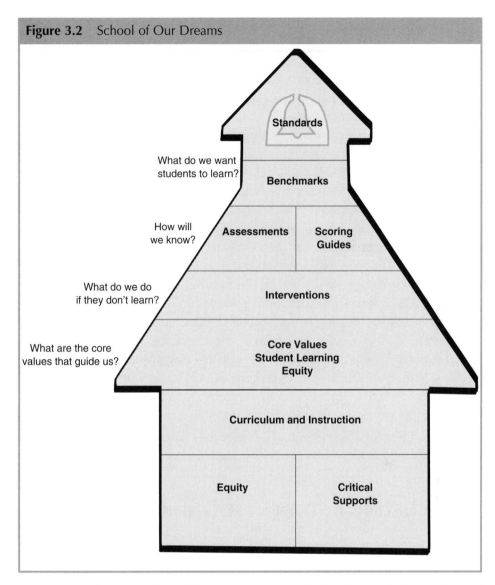

SOURCE: From *The Data Coach's Guide to Improving Learning for All Students: Unleashing the Power of Collaborative Inquiry* (CD-ROM, Resource R4.5), by N. Love, K. E. Stiles, S. Mundry, and K. DiRanna, 2008, Thousand Oaks, CA: Corwin Press. Reprinted with permission.

Vignette

Canton City Middle School Mathematics Data Team Aligns Curriculum With Standards

This vignette, written by Pam Bernabei-Rorrer, mathematics and Data Coach in Canton City, Ohio, illustrates how one Data Team built part of their foundation by getting clear about the knowledge they wanted students to acquire and aligning their curricula with standards. They made the critical shift from basing their curricula on textbooks to basing it on standards. This laid the foundation for using common benchmark assessments to measure progress toward their now-clarified learning goals.

The first leg of our journey focused on designing and implementing grade-level curriculum maps based on the newly created Ohio mathematics standards in 2002. Teachers came together in grade-level teams and dialogued about the meaning of the grade-level indicators. The result of the dialogue was a curriculum map broken into concept chunks for each of the four quarters of the school year. The mathematics curriculum in Canton City was no longer determined by the chapters in the textbook, but had a sensible flow allowing students to build upon their previous learning. After establishing curriculum maps for each grade, representatives from each grade level met to analyze the vertical alignment of the maps. The teachers examined the vertical flow of the curricula between the grades and evaluated the depth of each concept that extended over several grades. A logical sequence was established not only for each course, but throughout the entire mathematics program.

Since the curriculum no longer followed the outline of the textbook, the next step was to align resources to support the concept chunks in the map. Canton City's textbooks were over ten years old and did not include chapters on some of the Ohio standards, especially the standards involving probability and data analysis. New textbooks weren't a possibility due to budget constraints, however, so the mathematics team's solution was to collect and share their resources from various sites, including activity books from the National Council of Teachers of Mathematics (NCTM) Navigation series, Web sites, and other sources. For concept chunks that were still weak in instructional materials, new lessons were created by the mathematics team utilizing Schlechty's (2002) strategies for designing engaging student work. A notebook compiling the team's work was created and distributed to the members of the mathematics department. This became the new textbook for the district, serving to support the established curriculum maps while also establishing ownership of instruction for the teacher.

2. IDENTIFYING A STUDENT-LEARNING PROBLEM

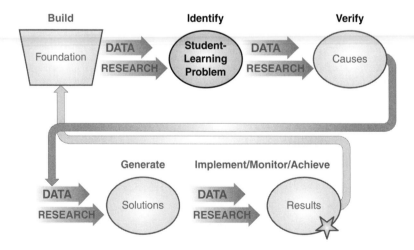

The second stage in the Using Data Process is Identifying a Student-Learning Problem. There are three major steps Data Teams take during this part of the process: (1) They drill down into multiple levels and sources of student-learning data, (2) synthesize findings, and (3) identify a student-learning problem and goal on which to focus improvement. During this stage of the process, Data Teams make use of collaborative tools for making sense of and talking about data together.

Identifying a Student-Learning Problem

- Drill down into multiple levels and sources of student-learning data
- Synthesize findings
- Formulate a student-learning problem statement and goal on which to focus improvement

---

The outcome of this stage is a clearly articulated student-learning problem that can be supported with evidence from multiple data sources, including student work, and a goal on which to focus improvement. Formulating a clear statement of the problem, detailing who the problem affects, what the problem is, and what achievement gaps are evident, is an important step toward improvement: it is hard to solve an ill-defined problem. A clear and measurable goal also gives the team a target to aim for and a way to monitor their progress. Otherwise, Data Teams are roaming aimlessly or trying to solve too many problems and accomplishing little. Finally, it is important that the problem and goal explicitly address improving the performance of historically underserved students so these students are not neglected yet again. In sum, attention to the steps in this stage of the process is the antidote to reliance on single and imperfect measures, failure to keep equity in the forefront, and the unclear goals that often doom improvement efforts.

Drill Down Into Multiple Levels and Sources of Student-Learning Data

The process of Identifying a Student-Learning Problem begins with drilling down into student-learning data—looking more and more deeply at one student-learning data source to derive the greatest possible amount of

When we looked at our state criterion-referenced tests [CRT] for sixth grade, life science was our weakest strand. We couldn't believe that. We thought we had a pretty strong life science program. It wasn't until we looked at our own local assessments and saw the same weakness that we became convinced that we had to take a closer look at what we were teaching and how.

—Kathy Porter, director of science, Canton City Schools, Canton, Ohio information from it. The drill-down moves through the following sequential layers of analysis:

- Aggregated level (largest group level)
- Disaggregated level (broken out by student populations, e.g. race/ethnicity, gender, poverty, language, mobility, and educational status)
- Strand level (content domains)
- Item level (student performance on each individual test item)
- Student work

> **Drilling Down Into Data:** Looking more and more deeply at one student-learning data source to derive the greatest possible amount of information. The drill-down moves through sequential layers of analysis, from the aggregated, disaggregated, strand, and item level to an analysis of student work.

When available and comparable, analysis of multiple years of student-learning data is recommended, as trends over time are more reliable than a single year of data. It is also useful, if possible, to have strand data, item-level data, and student work disaggregated by race/ethnicity, language, economic level, and educational status (special education).

Table 3.1 illustrates these levels of the drill-down, which can be conducted on any assessment for which they are available. As shown in the third column of the table, each level of data lends itself to answering specific questions about student learning and contributes to the Data Team's understanding of how well students are learning, which students are learning, and what content they are learning. In the Using Data Process, the Data Team drills down into state assessment data as well as common benchmark assessments and other sources of student-learning data. Since not all data sources are available at all levels, Data Teams make the best use of the sources and levels that are available to them.

As they drill down into multiple sources, Data Teams are asking

- What can and can't we compare across data sources? (Different tests frequently define content strands differently. Use the test blueprints that delineate the specific outcomes and skills within strands and examine individual test items to determine these distinctions so you know whether you are comparing "apples to apples" or "apples to oranges.")
- What patterns or trends are we seeing?
- Is the problem with student learning we are seeing in one data source also evident in another? Why or why not?
- What new insights are we gaining into student understanding?

Table 3.1   Drilling Down Into Multiple Levels of Student-Learning Data

Level of Data	Example
Aggregated data	Number and Percentage of Students At and Above Proficiency in Sixth-Grade Mathematics on State CRT, Years 1–3 (School, District, State) Questions to ask: How do our students perform in comparison to schools at the district and state level, and to similar schools if data are available? What trends over time do we observe? To what extent are we meeting our students' learning needs through our school program?
Disaggregated data	Percentage of Students At and Above Proficiency by Race/Ethnicity in Tenth-Grade Mathematics on State CRT, Years 1–3 (School) Questions to ask: Are there achievement gaps between different groups of students? To what extent have these gaps changed over time? How can we better serve *all* of the students in our school?

For the aggregated data table:

Exam year	School ◇		District ▣		State △	
	#	%	#	%	#	%
1	235	62	859	59	78,233	80
2	237	68	902	52	80,342	79
3	256	55	989	45	82,099	72

For the disaggregated data table:

Racial/Ethnic Group	#	%	#	%	#	%
White ▣	266	82	226	81	250	86
African American ◆	159	49	165	52	135	60
Latino/a ▲	29	25	45	38	52	39

☐ Go! (green)   ☐ Caution! (yellow)   ☐ Urgent! (red)

Table 3.1 (Continued)

Level of Data	Example
Strand data	*(see table below)*

PERCENTAGE CORRECT ON FOURTH-GRADE LANGUAGE ARTS STRANDS, YEARS 1–3

Year of Test	Year 1	Year 2	Year 3
Number of Students Tested	87	101	98
Languages Arts Strands	% Correct	% Correct	%Correct
Language	55	58	62
Reading/Literature	53	53	60
Topic Development	43	46	46
Conventions	68	67	70
Writing	50	55	53

Questions to ask:

What content strands are being assessed?

What skills and concepts are being assessed within each strand?

What are areas of relative strength and weakness in our students' performance on content strands?

Level of Data	Example
Item-level data	*(see table below)*

ITEM ANALYSIS FOR SIXTH-GRADE MATHEMATICS STRAND "NUMBERS AND NUMBER RELATIONS"

S = Short Answer (2 possible points)

Proficient = 2

E = Extended Response (4 possible points)

Proficient = 3 or 4

TEST PART	STRAND	OUTCOME #	ITEM #	CORRECT ANSWER	A – 0	B – 1	C – 2	D – 3	4	BLANK	BLDG %	DIST %	STATE %	N= BLDG
M	NU	10	1	C	15	23	49	12	0	0	49	48	62	282
M	NU	10	7	S	47	32	12	0	0	10	12	9	20	282
M	NU	06	16	0	4	7	4	85	0	0	85	81	87	282
M	NU	07	19	S	47	15	28	0	0	9	28	23	45	282
M	NU	08	20	D	6	27	11	56	0	0	56	59	73	282
M	NU	06	22	B	16	38	26	20	0	1	38	37	53	282
M	NU	09	35	D	50	10	33	17	0	0	17	25	40	282
M	NU	08	41	D	9	12	39	37	0	3	37	27	44	282
M	NU	06	45	B	33	50	8	4	0	6	50	48	58	282
M	NU	09	39	E	6	60	20	3	3	9	6	7	17	282

Adapted from the Ohio Department of Education, data reporting table for student item-level test data, 2003. Used with permission of the Ohio Department of Education.

Questions to ask:

What kinds of items are on the assessment? In what content area? At what level of difficulty?

What specific skills and understandings are our students' strengths? Which pose difficulties?

On what types of questions, such as short answer, extended response, or multiple-choice, do our students perform well? Which pose difficulties?

Why are our students doing well or missing points on their open-response questions?

Table 3.1 (Continued)

Level of Data	Example
Student work	**Open-Ended Prompt** Please write (or draw) your answer directly on the lines or in the space provided. • You are the owner of a company that supplies local florists with tulips. Last year the tulips you produced tended to be smaller than usual and you wonder if it had something to do with the soil temperature in the winter. • You recorded the ground temperature where the tulip bulbs were dormant and the average height of the plants when they sprouted. Your data chart looks like this:

HEIGHT OF TULIP PLANTS
ONE WEEK AFTER BREAKING THROUGH SOIL

	AREA A	AREA B	AREA C
Ground Temperature in Winter	7 C	2 C	0 C
Average Height of Plants	4 cm	8 cm	14 cm

1. Graph the data on the grid below. Remember to label the graph.

2. Based on the data from the graph, describe the relationship between ground temperature in winter and the height of tulip plants after a week of visible growth.

The relationship is the more the temperature goes down the height gets taller.

SOURCE: Adapted from the Fall 2004 Partnership for Student Success in Science student assessment. Designed by Dr. Shavelson of Stanford University. Reprinted with permission.

Questions to ask:

What skills, knowledge, and concepts do students have mastery or understanding of as evidenced by their work?

Are our observations and inferences from other levels of data validated by the student work? If not, how do we explain our findings?

What additional insights have we gained about student thinking?

SOURCE: Examples from *The Data Coach's Guide to Improving Learning for All Students: Unleashing the Power of Collaborative Inquiry* (Tasks 6–10), by N. Love, K. E. Stiles, S. Mundry, and K. DiRanna, 2008, Thousand Oaks, CA: Corwin Press. Reprinted with permission.

Having Data Conversations: Data-Driven Dialogue

Teachers are often handed reams of data or a computer program that slices and dices data every which way and are directed to use those data to improve instruction—but little happens. This is not unlike handing students a science textbook and saying, "Read this and learn science." What is missing is the opportunity for constructing meaning, making sense, and engaging in meaningful dialogue. Effective collaborative inquiry takes what we know about how people learn and applies it to data analysis. It also provides opportunities for personal reflection on assumptions, beliefs, and values, and for strengthening cultural proficiency as a critical lens to bring to data interpretation.

> *Until teachers started talking deeply about the data, they would create plans that never got implemented. The best thing about the Using Data [Process] is that it engages teachers in deep discussions of data.*
>
> —Richard Dinko, former coprincipal investigator, Stark County Mathematics and Science Partnership, Canton, Ohio

The Using Data Process incorporates over thirty tools to help Data Teams learn about, organize, display, analyze, talk about, and act on data. One such tool at the heart of the Using Data Process is Data-Driven Dialogue, a structured approach to talking about data (see Figure 3.3). Adapted from a model developed by Bruce Wellman and Laura Lipton (2004), Data-Driven Dialogue is "steeped in current understandings about how we learn" (p. 43). A valuable tool for the drill-down process, Data-Driven Dialogue can also be used with other kinds of data, including survey or observation data, which are analyzed elsewhere in the Using Data Process.

Data-Driven Dialogue applies what is known about how learners make sense of new knowledge through activating prior knowledge, using vibrant

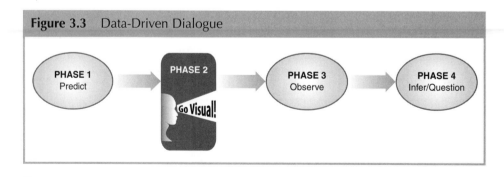

Figure 3.3   Data-Driven Dialogue

SOURCE: Adapted from *Data-Driven Dialogue: A Facilitator's Guide to Collaborative Inquiry*, by L. Lipton and B. Wellman, 2004, Sherman, CT: Mira Via, LLC. For additional information, go to www.miravia.com. Reprinted with permission.

NOTE: This figure is also used in *The Data Coach's Guide to Improving Learning for All Students: Unleashing the Power of Collaborative Inquiry* (p. 73), by N. Love, K. E. Stiles, S. Mundry, and K. DiRanna, 2008, Thousand Oaks, CA: Corwin Press.

visual displays, opening up extended opportunities for exploration and discovering, and engaging in dialogue about assumptions. The learners in this case are the Data Team members, and the source of their new knowledge is the data they will be examining. The process has four phases:

- *Phase 1: Predict.* Data Team members surface their assumptions and predictions about what they think they will see in the data before looking at them.
- *Phase 2: Go Visual.* The team examines simple, large, colorful, and often hand-drawn displays of data that the entire team can look at together.
- *Phase 3: Observe.* The team members set aside their interpretations and assumptions and focus only on what is there to be observed in the data.
- *Phase 4: Infer/Question.* The team generates interpretations for the results they observe, generating multiple possible explanations or implications for what they are seeing.

By surfacing assumptions first and then separating observations of data from interpretations, participants in Data-Driven Dialogue learn to critically examine their assumptions and broaden their perspectives before taking action. This can be especially important in examining how our cultural biases shape our data interpretations.

Data-Driven Dialogue: A four-phase process for talking about and making sense of data by (1) activating prior knowledge and surfacing assumptions (Predict); (2) using vibrant visual displays (Go Visual); (3) opening up extended opportunities for exploration and discovery (Observe); and (4) generating possible explanations, inferences, and questions about the data (Infer/Question; Love et al., 2008; Wellman & Lipton, 2004).

Synthesize Findings

Once the Data Team has drilled down into multiple measures and levels of student-learning data, they synthesize their findings. This is the second step in Identifying a Student-Learning Problem. As Data Teams "walk across" their multiple sources and levels of data, they look for patterns and connections across all the data and for a verified student-learning problem, evident in more than one data source. See Figure 3.4 for

Figure 3.4 Identifying a Student-Learning Problem: Summary of Findings

Content Area	Science		Grade Level	Sixth grade

	Types of Data		
	1: _____ State CRT _____	2: Classroom performance task on floating and sinking (4–0 point scoring rubric)	3: District common benchmark assessment in physical science (multiple-choice and open-response)
Levels of data	Years: 2004–2006	Years: 2005–2006	Years: 2005–2006
Aggregated results	52 percent of sixth-grade students were proficient in science, a 2 percent decrease from last year	65 percent of all sixth-grade students scored a rubric rating of 2 or below	60 percent of all sixth-grade students passed the physical science assessment
Disaggregated results	There is a persistent achievement gap between White and Latino/a students in science; this year's gap was 38 percentage points	Of the students who scored a rubric rating of 2 or below, 70 percent were Latino/a and 52 percent were White	There was an achievement gap of 28 percentage points between White and Latino/a students
Strand results	For two years, the lowest percentage of students were proficient in the physical science strand: 31 percent last year, 28 percent this year	N/A (the assessment focused on one strand area)	N/A (the assessment focused on one strand area)
Item analysis	Of the eight physical science multiple-choice items, students performed worst on the three items pertaining to floating and sinking, with 23–30 percent proficient	Students performed poorly on the part of the task that required them to explain why objects floated or sank	Students performed most poorly on the ten items assessing buoyancy, with an average of 22 percent proficient; six of these items asked students to predict which objects would either float or sink
Student work	N/A (no state data provided)	Showed evidence of student misconceptions of the relationship between an object's composition and its buoyancy; students consistently relied on the object's size to determine its buoyancy	Showed evidence of misconceptions with the concept of buoyancy and of how the composition of an object relates to its buoyancy
Student-learning problem:			

SOURCE: From *The Data Coach's Guide to Improving Learning for All Students: Unleashing the Power of Collaborative Inquiry* (p. 230), by N. Love, K. E. Stiles, S. Mundry, and K. DiRanna, 2008, Thousand Oaks, CA: Corwin Press. Reprinted with permission.

an example of one Data Team's summary of their findings from analyzing state criterion-referenced tests, their own local classroom performance task, and common course assessments.

Sample Observations From a Walk Across the Data

- Mathematics problem solving shows up consistently as a weak area in our state and local assessments.
- Across the board, our students perform more poorly in reading comprehension with nonfiction than fiction.
- There is a pattern across all the data in statistics and probability. This is the lowest strand on our state and common assessments.
- Achievement gaps between our White and African American students are evident in our state as well as our district assessments.

Formulate a Student-Learning Problem Statement and Goal

Formulating a problem statement and goal is the last step in the Identifying a Student-Learning Problem stage and the culmination of the team's engagement with multiple sources and levels of student-learning data. Now they prioritize the problems that surfaced in the data, choose one problem to focus on, and articulate an accompanying student-learning goal. They take the time to articulate a problem statement so that they are clear who has the problem, what specific content strand or concept or skill is the problem, and what achievement gaps are evident—all based on evidence.

Student-Learning Problem Statement Example

Sixth-grade students at Lincoln Elementary School are below proficiency in science. A weak strand is physical science, particularly in buoyancy, as evidenced by these data:

- 52 percent of students were proficient on last year's state science CRT; 28 percent were proficient in the physical science strand.
- 65 percent of students scored a rubric rating of 2 or below on this year's school-administered performance task on floating and sinking.
- 60 percent of students passed the most recent district common benchmark assessment in physical science.
- 23 to 30 percent of students were proficient on test items relating to buoyancy on last year's state CRT; students also performed poorly on items relating to buoyancy on the other two data sources.

(Continued)

(Continued)

Within this subject area a performance gap was noted between White and Latino/a students as evidenced by these data:

- There was an achievement gap of 38 percentage points on last year's state CRT.
- 52 percent of White students scored a rubric rating of 2 or below on this year's school-administered floating and sinking performance task, compared to 70 percent of Latino/a students.
- There was an achievement gap of 28 percentage points on the most recent district common benchmark assessment in physical science.

SOURCE: From *The Data Coach's Guide to Improving Learning for All Students: Unleashing the Power of Collaborative Inquiry* (p. 242), by N. Love, K. E. Stiles, S. Mundry, and K. DiRanna, 2008, Thousand Oaks, CA: Corwin Press. Reprinted with permission.

Once the problem is clearly defined, formulating a goal is easy. The goal is the problem solved. Depending upon their role, Data Teams set a goal for their school and/or a grade level or course. Individual teachers can also work with each student to identify his or her individual student-learning goal as well. Effective goal statements are achievable and include enough information so that you will know when you have achieved them. Data Teams set SMART goals, which meet the following criteria:

Specific: The goal identifies what will happen and with whom.

Measurable: The goal includes clear indicators of success.

Attainable: The goal can be accomplished with the strengths, abilities, and resources available.

Relevant: There is a documented need for the goal and it is something you want to do.

Time-Bound: The goal includes the time frame for when it will be met.

Using Data Process developers learned that goal setting can be an iterative process. At this stage, the team may be ready for a simple goal statement—what we want by when, a "sort-of-SMART" goal—but lack detailed indicators of success. Some teams find it hard to be specific about the numerical results to be achieved on various assessments, especially if they do not yet know how they will tackle the goal or have not yet studied monitoring. See the sample of a first-draft goal statement provided below. The team can revisit their goal later, when developing the monitoring plan, making it SMARTer by adding the specific indicators to be monitored (see Figure 3.7 later in the chapter).

Draft Student-Learning Goal Statement Example: By next year we will improve sixth-grade students' learning in physical science and narrow achievement gaps between White and Latino/a students.

3. VERIFYING CAUSES

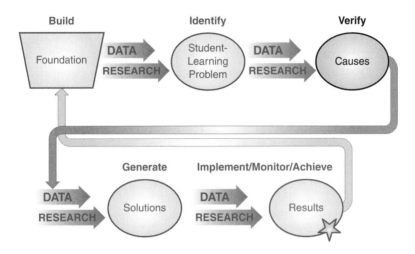

The third stage of the Using Data Process, Verifying Causes, is a critical part of our model that is often omitted in other improvement processes. It is the part of the process where you "look before you leap": the Data Team takes the time to examine relevant research as well as data about their own practice before developing an action plan. The goal is to make sure that the causes that are to be acted upon are in fact supported in research and focused on policies, practices, and beliefs that are within educators' control to act upon—not focused on blaming students or their circumstances. It

> *We learned that we needed to look at what . . . would make the most impact on students—instructional practice.*
>
> —Eileen Armelin, Data Coach and teacher, San Carlos Junior High School, San Carlos, Arizona

is also important that the causes identified are grounded in teachers' understanding of the content that students are struggling with and in the research about how to best help students learn that content.

During our work with schools, we observed Data Teams that were quite proficient at using data to identify student-learning problems but would often respond to those problems prematurely, before they explored fully what practices in their system might be contributing to the problem and what research has to say about that problem. For example, as you can read in the Katz Elementary School case study in Chapter 6, the Data Team accurately identified that their students had difficulty solving nonroutine mathematics problems. They concluded that the cause of this student-learning problem was that students were not persisting and that they were unable to read the problems. It wasn't until they actually observed forty students engaged in problem solving that they saw that their theory didn't hold water. Students were persisting. And even when the problem was read aloud to the students, they still weren't able to solve it. Through their observations and by consulting research, the team ultimately came to the conclusion that the cause of the problem was that students lacked problem-solving strategies, not persistence. This led to a very different course of action.

The Using Data Process builds in checks and balances to guide Data Teams to verify their causes with research and local data. There are three important steps in this stage: First, the Data Team generates multiple possible causes of the student-learning problem. Then they gather additional evidence to verify the causes through research. Finally, they collect and analyze local data about school and classroom practices to verify that the causes under consideration are of concern in their school. The Verify Causes Tree, shown in Figures 3.5 and 3.6, is a graphic organizer for the process; this is described in more detail below.

Verifying Causes

- Generate multiple possible causes for the student-learning problem
- Gather and study relevant research
- Collect and analyze local data about school and classroom practices

---

Generate Multiple Possible Causes for the Student-Learning Problem

It is important to cast the net broadly when generating causes, as most student-learning problems have multiple causes related to curriculum, instruction, assessment practices, equity (including opportunities to learn and beliefs about students), and critical supports (such as teacher preparation and professional development). Once multiple causes are generated, the team prioritizes which causes to further investigate, considering the following questions:

- Is the stated cause based on assumptions that blame any person or group of persons?
- Have we considered how our own weaknesses in understanding the content might contribute to the student-learning problem? How our instructional practices might contribute to it?

- Have we considered systemic causes?
- Which of these causes are within our control to act upon?
- Which causes are closer to the "proficiency" end of the Cultural Proficiency Continuum (see Chapter 4)?
- Which causes can have the greatest impact on solving the student-learning problem?
- Which causes can be verified with additional data and research?
- Which causes can be addressed given our resources and time constraints?

Figure 3.5 illustrates an example of one Data Team's prioritized possible causes. Note that initially, in this example, some of the possible causes under consideration were contradictory (e.g., "classes are too heterogeneous" and "tracking"). At this stage, that is fine. The Data Team will further investigate all causes and determine which, if any, to eliminate.

Gather and Study Relevant Research

A second crucial step in Verifying Causes is consulting research. At this stage, the team is asking whether research validates their cause (e.g., "Does tracking contribute to achievement gaps between White and African American students?" and "Does inclusion have a positive effect on students with exceptional needs?"). They are also seeking to learn more from research about this cause (e.g., "What class size is optimal for students?" and "What are the best practices for helping students master proportional reasoning?"). Then they gather research to answer their questions, considering the following guidelines:

- Is the author an authority on the subject? Has he or she contributed empirical work on the subject? Have others based their work on this author's work?
- When was the material written? (More recent materials reflect the most up-to-date information.)
- What was written about or tested? Does the material contain research that supports your needs?
- Does the source provide a well-designed study? A thoughtful analysis? An original way of viewing the topic?
- Does it meet U.S. Department of Education guidelines for scientific studies?

In the completed Verify Causes Tree example in Figure 3.6, the Data Team consulted a combination of secondary and primary sources and summarized their findings in the second row of the matrix. Note that on

Figure 3.5 Verify Causes Tree With Possible Causes

Student-Learning Problem	Sixth-grade students at Nevazoh Middle School are performing below proficiency in mathematics. A weak strand is mathematics problem solving. There is an achievement gap of 37 percent between White and African American students on state CRTs in sixth-grade mathematics in 2006–2007.			
	Curriculum	**Instruction**	**Assessment**	**Equity**	**Critical Supports**
Possible Causes	Does not emphasize mathematics problem solving enough	Classes are too heterogeneous		Tracking; lower-track students get more drill and practice	Teachers do not feel prepared to teach nonroutine problem solving
Research Findings					
Local Data Findings					
Verified Causes					

SOURCE: Adapted from *Root Cause Analysis: School Leader's Guide to Using Data to Dissolve Problems*, by P. G. Preuss, 2003, Larchmont, NY: Eye on Education. Reprinted with permission.

NOTE: This figure is also used in *The Data Coach's Guide to Improving Learning for All Students: Unleashing the Power of Collaborative Inquiry* (p. 256), by N. Love, K. E. Stiles, S. Mundry, and K. DiRanna, 2008, Thousand Oaks, CA: Corwin Press.

Figure 3.6   Completed Verify Causes Tree

Student-Learning Problem: Sixth-grade students at Nevazoh Middle School are performing below proficiency in mathematics. A weak strand is mathematics problem solving. There is an achievement gap of 37 percent between White and African American students on state CRTs in sixth-grade mathematics in 2006–2007.

	Curriculum	Instruction	Assessment	Equity	Critical Supports
Possible Causes[a]	Does not emphasize mathematics problem solving enough	~~Classes are too heterogeneous~~ Not using best practices consistently		Tracking	Teachers do not feel prepared to teach nonroutine problem solving
Research Findings	Rigorous curriculum benefits students and narrows achievement gaps (NRC, 2005; Singham, 2003)	Heterogeneous groupings with differentiated instruction, flexible groupings, extra help for students, and varied instructional approaches that build on students' understandings are recommended (NCTM, 2000; NRC, 2005; Oakes, 1993)		Tracking has a negative impact on students in low tracks, who receive less rigorous curriculum and less effective instruction; African American students are disproportionately represented in low tracks (Oakes, 1993; Singham, 2003)	Teacher preparation is an important factor in student achievement (Ma, 1999; NCTM, 2000; NRC, 2005; Singham, 2003)
Local Data Findings	Problem solving emphasized more in advanced mathematics classes, less in regular mathematics classes (observation and student interview data)	Best practices more in evidence in advanced mathematics classes (observation and student interview data)		11 percent of African Americans are enrolled in advanced math versus 44 percent of Whites; 75 percent of students in advanced mathematics classes scored proficient in mathematics compared with 10 percent of students in regular mathematics; 82 percent of African Americans in advanced mathematics scored proficient (enrollment and most recent state CRT data)	Most teachers report feeling "somewhat" or "inadequately" prepared to teach mathematics on most dimensions of preparation surveyed (teacher survey)
Verified Causes	Lack of emphasis on problem solving, especially in regular mathematics classes	Not using best teaching practices consistently, especially in regular mathematics classes		Tracking	Teachers do not feel prepared to teach nonroutine problem solving

SOURCE: Adapted from *Root Cause Analysis: School Leader's Guide to Using Data to Dissolve Problems*, by P. G. Preuss, 2003, Larchmont, NY: Eye on Education. Reprinted with permission.

a. Possible causes that are shaded indicate that they were maintained or added after studying research; cause that is crossed out was determined not to be confirmed by research.

NOTE: This figure is also used in *The Data Coach's Guide to Improving Learning for All Students: Unleashing the Power of Collaborative Inquiry* (p. 267), by N. Love, K. E. Stiles, S. Mundry, and K. DiRanna, 2008, Thousand Oaks, CA: Corwin Press.

the basis of their research findings, they eliminated heterogeneous groups as a possible cause and replaced it with "not using best practices consistently." Possible causes that are shaded indicate that they were maintained or added after studying research.

Collect and Analyze Local Data About School and Classroom Practices

Once the Data Team has verified their possible causes with research, they generate questions about their own local practice and collect and analyze local data, such as survey, interview, enrollment, or classroom observation data. Local data provide evidence of what is happening in the school in relationship to each cause, allowing the Data Team to verify that the cause is not only supported by research, but is also of concern in their own school. For example, they may have a hunch that teachers are not fully implementing their mathematics curriculum but need more data to determine to what extent the curriculum is being implemented as intended. In the example of the completed Verify Causes Tree, the Local Data Findings row illustrates the type of data the team collected and their summary findings.

While Verifying Causes is time-consuming, it ultimately saves time by ensuring that they don't pursue the wrong problem. They can now act with confidence on their verified causes, which become the basis for the solutions they will generate in the next part of the process.

4. GENERATING SOLUTIONS

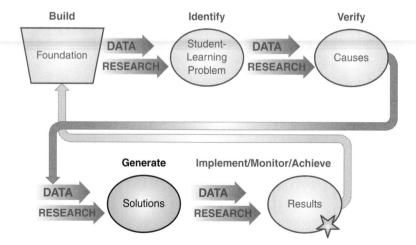

In Generating Solutions, the fourth stage of the Using Data Process, the Data Team plans how they will solve the student-learning problem they identified earlier, address their verified causes, and achieve their student-learning goal. In this part of the process, the team uses a Logic Model—a graphic representation of the logical and sequential steps involved in moving from their strategies to their desired goal (see an example of a Logic Model in Figure 3.7). As they develop the Logic Model, the Data Team asks these questions: (1) What strategies will we implement to address the verified causes and achieve the student-learning goal? (2) What outcomes do we expect to achieve along the way that will pave the way to achieving our student-learning goal? (3) How will we know if we have met our outcomes and achieved the student-learning goal? While we will discuss each of these questions sequentially, developing a Logic Model is a much more iterative process, with multiple entry points and opportunities to go back and refine answers to any of the above questions.

Generating Solutions Using a Logic Model

- What strategies will we implement to address the verified causes and achieve the student-learning goal?
- What outcomes do we expect to achieve along the way that will pave the way to achieving our student-learning goal?
- How will we know if we have met our outcomes and achieved the student-learning goal?

Logic-model thinking is rigorous intellectual work, but it is critically important in preventing three prevalent problems in continuous-improvement efforts:

- Grabbing at strategies that never lead to that elusive student-learning goal
- Lack of clarity about intended outcomes
- Failure to monitor implementation of both results and actions

For example, a Data Team might decide that having a workshop on science content will improve their teaching. But they are missing a step—how to translate that new content knowledge into their teaching, which will require ongoing practice with coaching and feedback. With logic-model thinking, Data Teams "lay the tracks," carefully thinking through their strategies and outcomes to prevent the improvement process from being derailed before achieving the intended results.

Figure 3.7 Using Data Process Logic Model Example

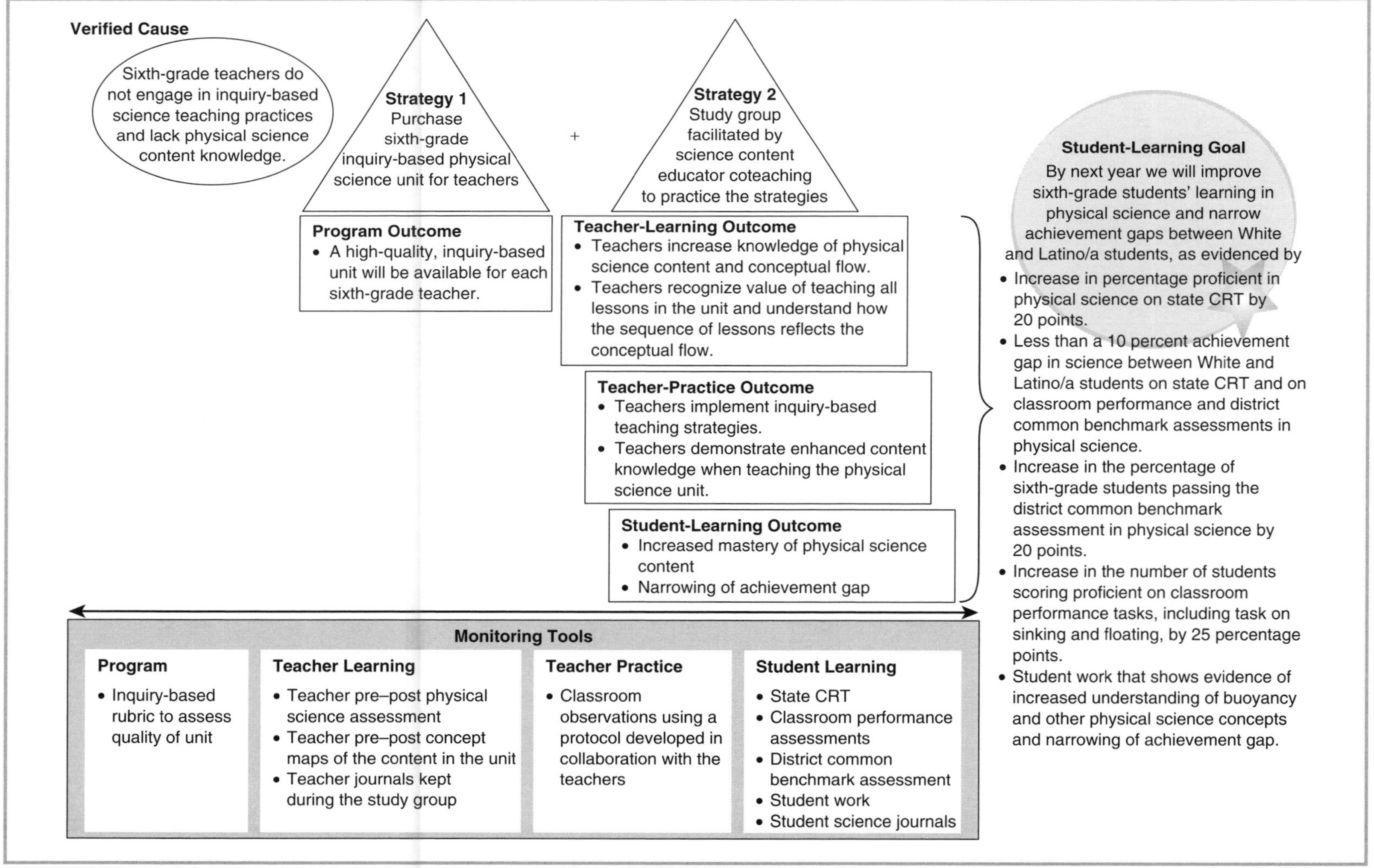

Verified Cause

Sixth-grade teachers do not engage in inquiry-based science teaching practices and lack physical science content knowledge.

Strategy 1
Purchase sixth-grade inquiry-based physical science unit for teachers

Program Outcome
- A high-quality, inquiry-based unit will be available for each sixth-grade teacher.

+

Strategy 2
Study group facilitated by science content educator coteaching to practice the strategies

Teacher-Learning Outcome
- Teachers increase knowledge of physical science content and conceptual flow.
- Teachers recognize value of teaching all lessons in the unit and understand how the sequence of lessons reflects the conceptual flow.

Teacher-Practice Outcome
- Teachers implement inquiry-based teaching strategies.
- Teachers demonstrate enhanced content knowledge when teaching the physical science unit.

Student-Learning Outcome
- Increased mastery of physical science content
- Narrowing of achievement gap

Student-Learning Goal
By next year we will improve sixth-grade students' learning in physical science and narrow achievement gaps between White and Latino/a students, as evidenced by
- Increase in percentage proficient in physical science on state CRT by 20 points.
- Less than a 10 percent achievement gap in science between White and Latino/a students on state CRT and on classroom performance and district common benchmark assessments in physical science.
- Increase in the percentage of sixth-grade students passing the district common benchmark assessment in physical science by 20 points.
- Increase in the number of students scoring proficient on classroom performance tasks, including task on sinking and floating, by 25 percentage points.
- Student work that shows evidence of increased understanding of buoyancy and other physical science concepts and narrowing of achievement gap.

Monitoring Tools

Program
- Inquiry-based rubric to assess quality of unit

Teacher Learning
- Teacher pre–post physical science assessment
- Teacher pre–post concept maps of the content in the unit
- Teacher journals kept during the study group

Teacher Practice
- Classroom observations using a protocol developed in collaboration with the teachers

Student Learning
- State CRT
- Classroom performance assessments
- District common benchmark assessment
- Student work
- Student science journals

SOURCE: From *The Data Coach's Guide to Improving Learning for All Students: Unleashing the Power of Collaborative Inquiry* (p. 300), by N. Love, K. E. Stiles, S. Mundry, and K. DiRanna, 2008, Thousand Oaks, CA: Corwin Press. Reprinted with permission.

What Strategies Will We Implement to Address the Verified Cause and Achieve the Student-Learning Goal?

While there are multiple entry points into the Logic Model, many people like to start with generating strategies—the specific activities the Data Team will implement to respond to the verified cause and that will lead to the achievement of the student-learning goal. The Data Team returns to what was learned from the research and local data to guide their thinking. For example, strategies might include working with the building administrator to eliminate tracking, adopting new instructional materials, conducting study groups or workshops to deepen teachers' content knowledge, implementing use of formative assessments, identifying and systematically offering extra help to students who need it, or providing coaching opportunities to help teachers practice specific skills. Often it is a combination of strategies, rather than any one strategy, which will lead to achieving a student-learning goal. The Logic Model in Figure 3.7 has two triangles to represent strategies, but Data Teams may have more.

Features of Strategies

- Have a clear purpose
- Can combine with other strategies
- Make a positive difference
- Can be monitored
- Are logically linked to the outcomes
- Are supported by research and best practice

What Outcomes Do We Expect to Achieve?

A logical next step in developing a Logic Model is to identify what the Data Team expects will happen as a result of the implementation of their strategies. The Logic Model focuses on four potential outcome areas:

- Program outcome: What do we expect to see as a result of changes in our content-area program, teaching, or educational policies?
- Teacher-learning outcome: What do we expect teachers to know, understand, believe, and/or be able to do?
- Teacher-practice outcome: What do we expect to see happening in classrooms in terms of teacher practice?
- Student-learning outcome: What do we expect students to know, understand, believe, and/or be able to do?

For example, a strategy to "conduct study groups focused on inquiry-based teaching and learning" might have an expected teacher-learning outcome that "teachers deepen their knowledge of inquiry-based approaches to teaching and learning" and a teacher-practice outcome that "teachers implement inquiry-based teaching strategies in their classrooms." It is important not to expect changes in student learning until changes in teacher practice are evident. The Logic Model in Figure 3.7 has boxes for each of the four outcome areas, with examples for each.

How Will We Know If We Have Met Our Outcomes and Achieved the Student-Learning Goal?

The next step in developing a Logic Model is to develop a plan for monitoring both implementation and results (see the Monitoring Tools boxes on the Logic Model example in Figure 3.7). The Data Team considers each of the outcomes they have defined. Then they think about what monitoring tools they will use to collect evidence—during and/or after implementation—of the extent to which each outcome has been met. For example, if one outcome in teaching practice is "teachers increase their use of open-response, higher-order thinking questions in the classroom," then teachers can monitor the amount of time each week they spend doing so and analyze their data together in the Data Team. The simple act of monitoring, in itself, builds accountability and momentum for the desired outcome. In fact, schools that were most successful in improving student achievement through the Using Data Project were those that regularly monitored student progress as strategies were being implemented, using data about their own instructional practices as well as about student learning. Developing a monitoring plan as part of their early planning sharpens the Data Team's thinking about their outcomes and strategies and helps ensure that monitoring will take place during implementation.

> *What gets measured gets done.*
>
> —Tom Peters (1987, p. 268)

Finally, Data Teams use the Logic Model to further refine their student-learning goal, adding the sources of evidence they will use to determine to what extent their ultimate goal has been met. These sources can include state assessment results as well as common benchmark assessment and quality of student work. A fully developed student-learning goal is illustrated in the example Logic Model (Figure 3.7).

5. IMPLEMENTING, MONITORING, AND ACHIEVING RESULTS

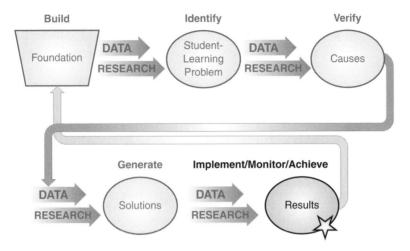

In this final stage of the Using Data Process, Data Teams flesh out and implement their action plans, gather data to monitor implementation and results, celebrate and disseminate successes, and renew their commitment to ongoing collaborative inquiry. Throughout this stage of the process, Data Team members will be wearing two hats—as implementers and as monitors. As implementers, they will be putting strategies into action in their own classrooms and/or providing the support and training for others to implement in their classrooms. As monitors, they will be gathering data that will be used to improve the action plan and determine whether outcomes are being met.

In essence, the Data Team engages in cycles of taking action, reflecting on the results, making adjustments, and taking new action. As they reach key milestones or benchmarks, they publicly recognize their success. They then reenter the cycle by asking, "Where do we go next? What other actions need to be taken to enhance student learning?" A challenge in this stage and throughout the process is balancing short cycles of improvement—based on frequent monitoring and changes in classroom practice—with long-term and larger-scale improvement efforts, such as curriculum implementation. The Using Data Process embraces both.

Implementing, Monitoring, and Achieving Results

- Take action and monitor results
- Celebrate success and renew commitment to collaborative inquiry
- Balance long- and short-term improvement

Take Action and Monitor Results

For over thirty years, educators have introduced innovations aimed at improving student outcomes. Yet time after time, professional development, curriculum adoptions, policy changes, and other interventions fail to be fully implemented because they lack follow-up and monitoring to assess whether the change has been made and whether it has had the desired effect on student learning. We cannot expect to see improvements in learning unless we know there have been changes in practice. This stage of the process is where the rubber meets the road. The Data Coach and Data Team are now responsible for ensuring that a set of coordinated actions designed to reach the intended outcome are launched and carefully monitored.

Monitoring Tips

- Do less, monitor more.
- Collect data about the teachers (instructional practice) as well as about students.
- Quantify your outcomes: How much have we improved? How often are we gathering data to assess our improvement?
- Assess multiple outcomes using one monitoring tool or process—go for multiple mileage!
- Ensure that diverse voices are included when gathering data through interviews, surveys, or focus groups.
- Be specific about what you want to learn (i.e., what evidence you want) before deciding on a monitoring tool.
- Measure what you treasure—make sure you are gathering data on outcomes that really matter!
- Keep equity in the forefront; disaggregate student-learning monitoring data by relevant student populations.

In this stage of the process, the team puts the monitoring plan they developed in the Generating Solutions stage into action. They collect and analyze data to learn what adjustments to make in the implementation of the action plan as well as determine when outcomes have been met. For example, if the action plan starts with a professional development program to enhance teachers' content knowledge, one set of monitoring data will focus on the quality of the program (e.g., gathered through observations of the sessions) and another on the extent to which teachers enhanced their content knowledge (e.g., gathered through pre- and postimplementation teacher assessments). The analysis of the monitoring data can help the Data Team know if the program that was provided was of the expected quality and whether it contributed to teachers' learning.

At this point, the Data Team is focused on the following questions:

- To what extent are the strategies being implemented?
- What barriers to implementation are we facing and how will we address them?
- Are the necessary skill, will, and resources in place to enable action?
- To what degree are we making progress toward our stated outcomes and student-learning goal?
- What should we do next? For example, what do we do if we don't achieve our results? If we are making progress, what additional intervention is needed? If we attain our outcomes, what can we do to sustain what's working? What new areas of improvement will we address next?
- How will we report and share our results and with whom?
- What will we celebrate? What and who will be rewarded and recognized? How will we celebrate?
- How will we sustain and renew our practice of using collaborative inquiry to ensure student learning?
- How will we amplify our successes and engage others in the Using Data Process?

Celebrate Success and Renew Commitment to Collaborative Inquiry

Throughout the Using Data Process, Data Teams share successes so that best practices spread throughout the members of the team and the school. But during this final stage of the Using Data Process it is time to determine to what extent the overall student-learning goal was met and to engage the whole community in celebrating accomplishments and sharing lessons learned. For example, the Using Data Project staff convened all the Data Teams in a district or project for annual portfolio presentations documenting the journey and the accomplishments of each Data Team. These celebrations help the teams renew their commitment to the collaborative inquiry process and plan for next steps, which might include examining new data and repeating the cycle, exploring other content areas or grade levels in need of improvement, or engaging more teachers in collaborative inquiry. Whichever path the Data Team takes, the overall goal is to sustain collaborative inquiry as the foundational process to guide the improvement of teaching and learning.

Canton City Middle School Mathematics Team Amplifies Success

On the Canton City Middle Schools Data Team, one teacher had particularly good results on the statistics and probability strand of the common benchmark assessment. He shared the materials he used with the students (adapted from his college statistics textbook!), and soon all the teachers in four middle schools were using those materials and improving their students' achievement in statistics.

Balance Long- and Short-Term Improvement

While advocating long-term capacity building, Michael Fullan (2005) also argues that "there is no excuse for failing to design and implement strategies that get short-term results" (p. 25). Short-term gains are motivating for teachers and build trust with the public. Long-term, systemic improvement is required to build capacity to sustain change over time, promote deep learning for students and teachers, and get all—not most—students achieving at high levels. While Data Teams are engaged in short cycles of improvement, regularly monitoring student progress and responding with instructional improvements in their classroom, they are simultaneously part of a larger, long-term, multiyear systematic improvement process under way at the school and district level. One does not negate the other.

Data Teams ask, "What short-cycle improvement actions can we take in our own classroom?" "What annual action plans can we put in place to improve our programs and our teaching?" At the same time, they coordinate with key administrators to implement larger-scale changes, such as curriculum implementation, establishment of professional learning communities, or wide-scale implementation of formative assessment strategies. Effective collaborative inquiry balances long- and short-term improvement.

SUMMARY

The Using Data Process is a successful model for collaborative inquiry that incorporates the following features, broadly applicable to any improvement process:

- Provides a structured process that can be adapted to local contexts
- Builds a solid foundation for collaborative inquiry by establishing shared values, vision, and parameters for Data Team work
- Emphasizes equity and cultural proficiency throughout the process
- Identifies a student-learning problem on which to focus improvement by analyzing multiple data sources

- Incorporates tools for sense-making and dialogue such as Data-Driven Dialogue
- Verifies causes of student-learning problems through use of research and local data about practice
- Generates solutions by drawing on research and best practice and using a Logic Model to link solutions to intended results
- Frequently monitors both implementation and results
- Celebrates and amplifies successes
- Attends to collaborative relationships and school culture
- Balances long- and short-term improvement
- Weaves in ongoing professional development for teachers

REFERENCES

Fullan, M. (2005). *Leadership and sustainability: System thinkers in action.* Thousand Oaks, CA: Corwin Press.

Lindsey, R. B., Roberts, L. M., & CampbellJones, F. (2005). *The culturally proficient school: An implementation guide for school leaders.* Thousand Oaks, CA: Corwin Press.

Love, N., Stiles, K. E., Mundry, S., & DiRanna, K. (2008). *The data coach's guide to improving learning for all students: Unleashing the power of collaborative inquiry.* Thousand Oaks, CA: Corwin Press.

Peters, T. (1987). *Thriving on chaos: A handbook for a management revolution.* New York: Knopf.

Preuss, P. G. (2003). *School leader's guide to root cause analysis: Using data to dissolve problems.* Larchmont, NY: Eye on Education.

Schlechty, P. C. (2002). *Working on the work: An action plan for teachers, principals, and superintendents.* San Francisco: Jossey-Bass.

Wellman, B., & Lipton, L. (2004). *Data-driven dialogue: A facilitator's guide to collaborative inquiry.* Sherman, CT: MiraVia.

Zuman, J. (2006). *Using Data Project: Final evaluation report.* Unpublished report. Arlington, MA: Intercultural Center for Research in Education.

4 Bringing Cultural Proficiency to Collaborative Inquiry

By Brenda CampbellJones,
Franklin CampbellJones, and Nancy Love

As consultants to the Using Data Project, Brenda CampbellJones and Franklin CampbellJones, leading experts and authors on cultural proficiency, helped developers integrate cultural proficiency as a prominent feature of the Using Data Process of Collaborative Inquiry (described in Chapter 3). In this chapter, the authors make the case that our cultural perspective shapes both our analysis of data and the actions taken beyond the data conversation. Becoming aware and changing our cultural assumptions when they negatively affect students is critically important work for those using data to guide improvement. The authors help us define two important concepts—culture and cultural proficiency—and provide us with both a conceptual framework and practical tools for bringing a culturally proficient perspective to data use and collaborative inquiry.

One of the most important actions educators can take to improve student learning is to develop their own understanding of culture and cultural proficiency and apply these understandings to their work.

Because culture is a predominant force in our lives, it shapes our values and assumptions. Those values and assumptions, in turn, shape the conversations we have about data and the actions we take as a result. An integral part of collaborative inquiry is for Data Teams to examine their own values and beliefs as they aim to better serve students whose cultures are different from their own. The purpose of this chapter is to explore the relationship between our cultural assumptions and our actions, discuss the concepts of culture and cultural proficiency, and show how Data Teams can take the journey toward cultural proficiency.

OUR ASSUMPTIONS SHAPE OUR DATA ANALYSIS AND OUR ACTIONS

Data Coach Dilemmas

Dilemma 1: A Data Team was looking at disaggregated student achievement data. One team member commented that this school was never going to be high-achieving because of the number of immigrant students. "These kids just don't value education or have much interest in learning," the team member remarked. The Data Coach was shocked but not sure how to address the situation. Should he allow the conversation to continue? Stop the group? Express his anger?

Dilemma 2: When generating causes of their student-learning problem, the team kept identifying causes that blamed the students and their circumstances: "Their parents don't value education." "They get no support at home doing their homework." "These kids know they are just going to work in the mine. How are we supposed to teach them mathematics?" "They just aren't motivated. Education is not a part of their culture." There was no discussion of their teaching or curriculum. The Data Coach knew these named causes were code words for racist and classist beliefs about their students. She struggled with how to shift the conversation away from these disrespectful and destructive comments and toward areas where the school could take action to improve learning opportunities for all students.

SOURCE: From *The Data Coach's Guide to Improving Learning for All Students: Unleashing the Power of Collaborative Inquiry* (p. 91), by N. Love, K. E. Stiles, S. Mundry, and K. DiRanna, 2008, Thousand Oaks, CA: Corwin Press. Reprinted with permission.

As the above dilemmas illustrate, our values and beliefs shape our interpretations of and reactions to data. Ultimately, these values and beliefs also determine the actions we take (Argyris, 1990). If, as in the first dilemma, one believes that immigrant students are not as capable as White, middle-class, American-born students, then achievement gap data only confirm the belief that such gaps are inevitable. There is no outrage and no constructive action to better serve immigrant children.

A pervasive belief in the culture of the United States is that children of color are less intelligent than their White peers, leading to low academic expectations of students of color among educators (Fashola, 2005; Kennedy, 2004). In particular, misperceptions about a student's science and mathematics abilities, coupled with attitudes about which students should access higher-level courses, shape actions taken by teachers, school counselors, and administrators that dramatically affect students' future lives. When such cultural biases remain unexamined and unchallenged, data do not lead to actions to improve learning opportunities for these students, but rather to blaming students and their circumstances for their failure, as in the second dilemma.

How Assumptions Lead to Action: The Ladder of Inference

Let's take a closer look at how our values and beliefs affect what data we select to see, the meaning we make of them, and the actions we take. Figure 4.1 illustrates the Ladder of Inference, a framework first developed by Chris Argyris (1990) and then expanded on by Peter Senge and his colleagues (Senge, Kleiner, Roberts, Ross, & Smith, 1994). The framework illustrates how strongly our beliefs determine our experience. The first rung of the ladder represents all the actual data and experience that would be captured by a movie camera that didn't lie. Based on our beliefs, we register some of those data while ignoring others. Then we impose our own meaning and interpretations on those data, develop assumptions, and draw conclusions from them. Our conclusions lead us to act in ways that reinforce our beliefs. In a reflexive loop, these beliefs, now often strengthened, further influence the data that we select. As the system becomes more and more closed and assumptions are not examined, we short-circuit reality and tend to think of our conclusions as the truth rather than as a sequence of leaps up the Ladder of Inference.

The example below shows how a teacher might move up the Ladder of Inference as she interacts with a student, ultimately taking action based on her own unexamined assumptions. Without checking out her assumptions and collecting more data from the student, she takes action that is harmful to the student based on a distorted picture of reality.

Step 1: I observe data as a video recorder would view it.

Example: On the first day of class, the teacher enters the room and observes that one of his students, Josh, has his head on the desk. This is the only observable data available to him.

Figure 4.1   Ladder of Inference

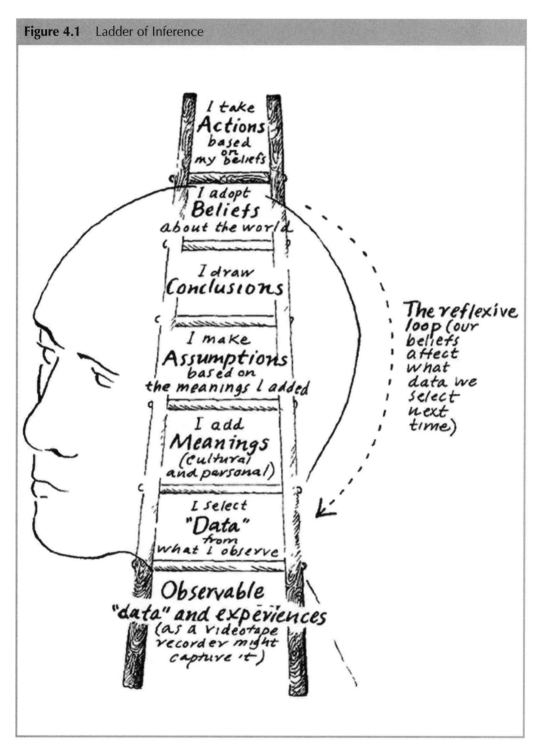

SOURCE: From *The Fifth Discipline Fieldbook: Strategies and Tools for Building a Learning Organization* (p. 243), by P. M. Senge, A. Kleiner, C. Roberts, R. B. Ross, and B. J. Smith, 1994, New York: Doubleday/ Currency. Reprinted with permission.

Step 2: I select data from what I observe.

Example: Based on Josh's posture, the teacher observes that the student appears to be asleep.

Step 3: I apply a culturally understood meaning to the data.

Example: The teacher gives this cultural meaning to the data: "Students who want to learn in my class stay engaged at all times." The teacher values engagement and obviously Josh is not engaged as his head is on the desk.

Step 4: I make assumptions based on the meaning.

Example: The teacher assumes, "Josh does not attend to his learning in a very energetic way."

Step 5: I draw conclusions.

Example: The teacher concludes that the student obviously doesn't want to learn in his class because he does not stay engaged while in the classroom setting.

Step 6: I adopt beliefs about the world.

Example: The teacher now believes that Josh and any student associated with him are not serious about school and most likely not good students.

Step 7: I take actions based on my belief.

Example: The teacher works to have Josh and any of his friends like him removed from his class.

Making assumptions and moving up the Ladder of Inference is something we all do. It happens so quickly and automatically, we rarely notice. Given the pervasiveness of cultural biases, however, it is critically important that we test out our assumptions for accuracy. For example, in Step 4 in the example above, the teacher makes an assumption about Josh's state of engagement as "unenergetic." The teacher could test this assumption by asking Josh about his physical state. Perhaps he works during the evenings to support his family, or maybe he is ill on this day. Josh's response to either of these questions could easily change the teacher's conclusion, affecting his belief and ultimately his actions.

The reflexive loop on the Ladder of Inference figure illustrates how the beliefs that we adopt actually determine what data we select for consideration. We pay attention to the data that support our beliefs and ignore those that contradict them. We can become effectively blind to data that are available to us in problem solving. For example, the teacher above would now scan for data to reinforce his belief that Josh is not a good student. In turn, Josh could react to the teacher by becoming even less engaged (going up his own ladder). Eventually, as beliefs become more rigid, each is paying attention to less and less reality. With untested assumptions, we come to think of our beliefs as "the" truth and view all others as false.

Data Teams can use the Ladder of Inference as a tool to become more aware of how their assumptions influence their data analysis and to further test out their assumptions before taking action based on them. Senge and colleagues (Senge et al., 2000) offer the following questions as a way to slow down conversations before participants charge up the ladder:

- What are the observable data behind that statement?
- Does everyone agree on what the data are?
- Can you run me through your reasoning?
- How did we get from that data to these abstract assumptions? (p. 70)

They also suggest that you can use the Ladder of Inference to help improve communications and results by

- becoming more aware of your own thinking and reasoning (reflection),
- making your thinking and reasoning more visible to others (advocacy),
- inquiring into others' thinking and reasoning (inquiry). (Senge et al., 1994, p. 245)

What Are Culture and Cultural Proficiency?

Just as our assumptions shape our understanding and actions, so our culture is a predominant force in shaping our assumptions. Culture is a powerful lens through which we select and interpret the data we observe and move up the Ladder of Inference. Stated another way, "you cannot not have culture" (Lindsey, Nuri-Robins, & Terrell, 2003, p. 160). Culture is

everything you believe and everything you do that enables you to identify with people who are like you and that distinguishes you from people who differ from you. Culture is about groupness. A culture is a group of people identified by their shared history, values, and patterns of behavior. (Lindsey et al., 2003, p. 41)

Much broader than just race and ethnicity, culture includes language, class, caste, gender, sexual orientation, geography, ancestry, physical and sensory abilities, occupation, and affiliation. It reflects the complex realities of individuals' identities. Understanding our own culture and how it affects us is an important step in expanding our perspectives to embrace and more accurately "see" those whose cultures differ from our own.

> **Culture:** "Everything you believe and everything you do that enables you to identify with people who are like you and that distinguishes you from people who differ from you" (Lindsey et al., 2003, p. 41).

Cultural proficiency is a way of being, a mindset that esteems one's own culture while positively engaging with those whose cultures differ from our own. It is "honoring the differences among cultures, viewing diversity as a benefit, and interacting knowledgeably and respectfully among a variety of cultural groups" (Lindsey, Roberts, & CampbellJones, 2005, p. xviii). Culturally proficient educators respect the culture of their students and place the students' cultural traits at the center of instruction and curricula rather than at the margins. A response of this nature calls on teachers to be cognizant of historical forces that place some students at the margins of curricula and instruction and to take effective action for providing a supportive environment that promotes rigorous academic achievement. It further requires teachers to know their culture, the culture of their students, and the role language plays in creating new realities (CampbellJones & CampbellJones, 2002; Lindsey et al., 2005).

As they develop and practice cultural proficiency, teachers, administrators, and counselors broaden their cultural lenses—seeing culture and its influence on us all, seeing privilege and its negative influence on learning, seeing students' cultures as a source of strength. They learn to reflect on their own beliefs and cultures by, for example, examining the effect that White privilege or racism has had on their lives. They actively seek alliances with people whose culture is different than theirs. For instance, a White male assistant principal made it his practice to move beyond his comfort zone and sit at the table where African American students gathered during lunch two to three days a week. At first, it was very awkward for him and the students. However, after a month of conversation with them and learning about their families, barriers between him and the students were eliminated. He learned about their culture. He knew their code words, which allowed him to move in and out of their circle quite freely. The students, in turn, learned to appreciate him and his cultural attributes as well. This assistant principal didn't stop there. He now sits at the gay and lesbian table with the same goals in mind. He plans to continue his journey toward cultural proficiency "one table at a time."

> **Cultural Proficiency:** "Honoring the differences among cultures, viewing diversity as a benefit, and interacting knowledgeably and respectfully among a variety of cultural groups" (Lindsey et al., 2005, p. xviii).

The Cultural Proficiency Continuum: A Tool for Cultural Proficiency

Developing cultural proficiency is an ongoing and essential part of the work of Data Teams, whose work it is to expand learning opportunities to more and more students. This requires looking at and transforming beliefs, interpretations of data, and practices that have acted as barriers to some students learning to their full potential. The Cultural Proficiency Continuum is one tool they can use to do so. The continuum is a framework for describing a range of six responses to diversity, from cultural destructiveness to cultural proficiency (see Figure 4.2):

- Cultural destructiveness: See the difference and stomp it out.
- Cultural incapacity: See the difference and make it wrong.
- Cultural blindness: See the difference and act like you don't.
- Cultural precompetence: See the difference and respond to it inappropriately.
- Cultural competence: See the difference that difference makes.
- Cultural proficiency: See the difference, respond positively, engage, and adapt.

Once familiar with the different points on the continuum, educators can be proactive in recognizing them, challenging assumptions, and facilitating deeper conversations about their responses to diversity. They can

Figure 4.2 The Cultural Proficiency Continuum

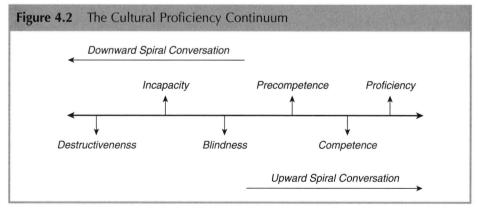

SOURCE: Adapted from *Cultural Proficiency: A Manual for School Leaders* (2nd ed; p. 85), by R. B. Lindsey, K. Nuri Robins, and R. D. Terrell, 2003, Thousand Oaks, CA: Corwin Press. Reprinted with permission.

Table 4.1   The Cultural Proficiency Continuum: Descriptions and Action

Point on the Continuum	Description	Action
Cultural destructiveness: See the difference and stomp it out.	Language and behavior at this point disparage, negate, or purge cultures that are different from your own.	Examples are genocide, ethnocide, eliminating historical accounts of cultures from school curricula, eliminating societal contributions of groups other than the dominant culture, including contributions in mathematics, science, art, and civics.
Cultural incapacity: See the difference and make it wrong. Elevate the superiority of your own cultural values and beliefs and suppress cultures that are different from your own.	Descriptive language at this point characterizes nondominant groups as less important or worthy than the dominant culture.	Includes lowered expectations for student groups, parents, and communities who are not or cannot be assimilated into the dominant culture.
Cultural blindness: See the difference and act like you don't. Act as if differences among cultures do not exist and/or refuse to recognize any differences.	The assumption at this point is that society is a meritocracy and that current and/or historical disparities between groups have been eliminated or never existed.	Proclamations of not seeing color in children or treating all children the same are commonplace.
Cultural precompetence: See the difference and respond inappropriately. Recognize that lack of knowledge, experience, and understanding of other cultures limits your ability to effectively interact with them.	Precompetent awareness signifies engagement in risk-taking behaviors aimed at dismantling the barriers of entitlement and nonadaptation. However, the responses are typically nonsystemic and haphazard, often requiring little or no change in regular school or classroom operations to meet the cultural needs of students.	Examples include quick fixes and short-term programs, delegation of diversity work to those who have been historically underserved or disenfranchised, and acknowledging culture superficially through events such as Black History Month.
Cultural competence: See the difference that difference makes. Interact with other cultural groups in ways that recognize and value their differences and motivate you to assess your own skills, expand your knowledge and resources, and ultimately cause you to adapt your relational behavior.	Competent behaviors include ongoing self-education and respectful responses to others while using the tools of cultural proficiency.	Actions include advocacy for others as equal participants and support for claims for social justice.
Cultural proficiency: See the difference, respond positively, engage and adapt. Honor the differences among cultures, seeing diversity as a benefit and interacting knowledgeably and respectfully among a variety of cultural groups.	Cultural proficiency entails an ever-evolving journey where one engages with and esteems the culture of another. Central is the acknowledgement of interdependence and the widening of friendships and allegiances, leading to personal and organizational transformation.	Examples include adaptation of curricula and pedagogical practices that place students' cultural attributes at the center of classroom learning. Reflecting upon the following questions before or after conducting a classroom lesson are features of this point on the continuum: Who is not being served well by this lesson? Who is at the margins as a result of this lesson? Who is at the center? What are ways of bringing those at the margins to the center of curricula and instruction?

SOURCE: Adapted from *Cultural Proficiency: A Manual for School Leaders* (2nd ed; pp. 85–91), by R. B. Lindsey, K. Nuri Robins, and R. D. Terrell, 2003, Thousand Oaks, CA: Corwin Press. Reprinted with permission.

consciously seek to move themselves further and further to the right of the continuum. Using the continuum effectively is like developing new eyes and ears—to see how cultural blindness and incapacity might be hampering the work of the Data Team. It can also be used to acknowledge, encourage, and celebrate growth toward cultural competence and proficiency.

The Downward Spiral Conversation

Table 4.1 elaborates on the Cultural Proficiency Continuum, including language and behaviors characterizing each point along the continuum. The first three points view the culture of others as deficient. Communication emanating within these points tends to be outward focused, blaming others for situations and circumstances. The conversation is usually about "them" or "those kids" and how they need to change or eradicate certain cultural attributes in order to assimilate into the dominant culture. Zander and Zander (2002) call such conversations "downward spiral conversations" in that they limit possibilities, stifle creativity, and don't lead anywhere. The vignette that follows illustrates a downward spiral conversation in a Data Team with members who are at the points of cultural destructiveness and cultural incapacity, reflecting little or no understanding of cultural proficiency.

Vignette ━━━

Part 1: Cultural Destructiveness and Incapacity and a Downward Spiral Conversation

We find the Data Team in the process of examining disaggregated test data provided to them by the district's research and evaluation department. Present at the meeting are Fredrick, the Data Team coach; Ray, a mathematics teacher; Debra, a school counselor; Raul, a physical education teacher; Erica, a biology teacher; and Marcia, the school's principal. As you read the vignette, pay attention to the language used to see what it may reveal about their beliefs about children. The team has been silently reviewing the data. They are now ready to respond to what they see in the data.

Fredrick: What do you read in the data? Remember to refrain from making inferences at this point. Look for observations and patterns.

Marcia: We have a huge gap in mathematics achievement between groups.

Raul: Yes, the African American, Latino, and Native American students seem to be lagging far behind our White students.

Marcia: Yes, our African American males have the lowest math scores.

Ray: Seems to me the data supports the fact that these kids can't cut it in math like regular kids can.

Debra: What do you mean by "these kids" and "regular kids"?

Ray:	Well, it's obvious these kids don't care. If they did, they would work harder like our kids who get good grades do.
Erica:	I can see Ray's point. Some kids just don't seem to have it when it comes to math. These kids seem to fit into that category. Ever since they put in those apartments nearby, our scores have gotten worse.
Ray:	Yeah, and if you check the enrollment data, you'll see that most of the African Americans live in those apartments.
Fredrick:	Perhaps we're jumping to conclusions too quickly. Let's get back to the data at hand. Are there any other patterns you see in the data that tells us something about student achievement?
Raul:	Well, it's not just the African American students we need to be concerned about. The socioeconomic status data shows that students on free-and-reduced lunch are having a difficult time also. Most of those kids live in the trailer parks.
Erica:	Perhaps our scores would improve when they rezone the district boundaries. I guarantee you if we get rid of the apartments and that trailer park, we'll have the highest scores in the district.
Ray:	Maybe we'll be lucky enough to get some Asian kids to help boost the scores of the American students.
Marcia:	Perhaps we need to slow down a bit and not stereotype our students.
Fredrick:	I think Marcia makes a good point. Let's try this another way.

This vignette characterizes a Data Team engaged at the left-hand side on the Cultural Proficiency Continuum, where some team members are unaware of how culturally destructive, incapacitating, and blind their attitudes and language are. At the heart of their cultural norms is the belief that only some children are capable of learning mathematics while others simply do not have the aptitude. What is more, some team members see these abilities along racial and class lines. Their perspectives ultimately lead to actions that affect curriculum offerings and instructional practices provided for students. Riddled with low expectations and stereotypical misconceptions of different group cultures, the views expressed by some members of the Data Team can easily drag the whole team into downward spiral conversation, blaming others rather than looking inward for solutions to problems. The best solution the team can offer for bolstering high academic student performance is to have the African American students and others residing in the trailer parks move away from the school's service area.

The Upward Spiral Conversation

The last three points on the Cultural Proficiency Continuum reflect growing cultural competence as policies, practices, and behaviors move toward ongoing reflection and assessment of culture and its impact, valuing diversity, managing dynamics constructively, and institutionalizing cultural knowledge (Lindsey et al., 2005). The blinders are lifted as educators begin to see differences as assets rather than as deficits. They are now poised to esteem the culture of others as well as their own. They recognize interdependence as normal and seek ways to bring each student's culture to the center of the curriculum. Moreover, the last three points on the continuum exemplify how we create our worldview through the choices we make in our use of language. An old axiom says, "If you believe you can, you are right. If you believe you can't, you are right." The same applies here. If you believe a child can achieve and help the child believe it, the child will achieve. As attitudes become more culturally proficient, conversations shift away from blaming others and toward taking internal responsibility for responding positively to students from diverse cultures. In this context, educators generate limitless possibilities for problem solving in upward spiral conversations (Zander & Zander, 2002).

What the authors have learned is that the perspective held by those analyzing the data will shape the tenor of the analysis and ultimately the actions they take beyond the data conversation. Let's revisit the Data Team in the vignette above after its members have advanced their knowledge of cultural proficiency. Although they are looking at the same data, they have now become cognizant of the continuum and are more skilled in monitoring their conversations so as not to blame students for achievement gaps. Rather, they look inward for solutions to advancing student learning.

Vignette

Part 2: Moving Toward Cultural Proficiency and the Upward Spiral Conversation

Fredrick: What do you see in the data?

Marcia: We have a huge gap in mathematics achievement between groups.

Raul: Yes, the African American, Latino, and Native American students are lagging far behind our White students.

Marcia: Yes. It appears that our African American males have the lowest math scores. Yet, with the gap, the students have gained a total of 15 percentage points over last year.

Ray: Yes, we are making gains, but the gap persists.

Fredrick: What are some inferences you are drawing at this point?

Debra: Maybe we are still serving these students poorly.

Erica: Wait a minute. I think that the data show that kids seem to be scoring differently depending on what level of mathematics they are taking. The kids in the higher-level course are mostly performing well, including the African American students. And I don't think it's just the case that a few African American kids are smart enough to take those courses. Maybe more kids should be taking higher-level mathematics.

Raul: I see the same pattern. If we had higher expectations for these students, I think they would perform better.

Ray:	Yes, the pattern just jumps out at you, doesn't it? I wonder what kind of instruction is going on in our higher-level courses compared to our lower-level courses. Should we even be offering these lower-level courses? What could we do to better prepare all our students for higher-level courses so they can be successful?
Raul:	As a follow-up to Ray's observation, it's not only the African American students we need to be concerned about. Our socioeconomic status data shows similar patterns. I wonder if our students living in poverty are getting the same opportunity to learn higher-level mathematics as other students.
Erica:	With all of our years of experience, I am positive we can respond to the needs of the children. I am convinced that we can bring the necessary skills to the table to enhance the learning of the students who are currently underserved.
Marcia:	Erica is right. It's my sincere belief that all children are capable of achieving our high academic standards in mathematics. We simply need to find a way to support their efforts—like looking at assessment data on a regular basis and giving extra help for students as they need it.
Fredrick:	Where would you like to take this investigation now?

This Data Team has progressed along the continuum from the first example. Having changed how they think about their students' cultures and capabilities, their language has changed accordingly. It is clear from the second conversation that the team members do not blame students for low test scores. Instead, they raise questions about how they may be underserving some students and leave themselves open for possible solutions to meet student needs that are well within their purview. They actively surface their beliefs when making inferences. Thus, they are poised for action that esteems the cultures of their students, placing these students front and center in all mathematics curricula and instructional decisions. They are now in an upward spiral conversation, generating possibilities and creating what they want to have happen.

USING CULTURAL PROFICIENCY CONCEPTS AND TOOLS WITH THE USING DATA PROCESS OF COLLABORATIVE INQUIRY

The above vignettes illustrate how a Data Team made a dramatic turnaround—from culturally destructive and downward spiral conversations to culturally competent and upward spiral conversations. What happens in between? How do educators make the journey to greater and greater cultural proficiency as they engage in collaborative inquiry? In our minds, the two go hand in hand—examining beliefs and assumptions is an integral part of engaging in collaborative inquiry to improve teaching and learning. Table 4.2 provides

Table 4.2 Integrating Cultural Proficiency and the Using Data Process

Stage of the Using Data Process	Ways to Integrate Cultural Proficiency
Building the Foundation	• Learn about cultural proficiency principles and the continuum. • Incorporate cultural proficiency into the vision for the school or program. • Establish group norms for talking about race/ethnicity, class, and culture. • Post the continuum on the wall every time the Data Team meets as a reminder.

Identifying a Student-Learning Problem	• Examine disaggregated data.
	• Reflect on inferences drawn from the disaggregated data by referring back to the continuum and asking:
	  o Do our inferences reflect cultural competence?
	  o If not, how can we reframe them?
	  o Is this an upward spiral or a downward spiral conversation?
	• Include achievement gaps in the student-learning problem and closing them as an explicit goal.

Verifying Causes	• Use the continuum as a filter for homing in on possible causes of student-learning problems by asking which of these causes:
	  o Are within our sphere of influence to act?
	  o Reflect understanding and respect for our students' diversity?
	  o Fall at the culturally proficient end of the continuum?
	• Dialogue about assumptions that underlie causes generated.
	• Test assumptions about causes with research and local data about practice using tools such as the Verify Causes Tree (see Chapter 3).
	• Talk to students and parents from different cultural backgrounds about how they perceive the causes of achievement gaps.
	• Learn about your students' cultures, prior knowledge and experience, and strengths before jumping to conclusions about causes.

Generating Solutions	• Reflect on the cultural proficiency of solutions generated by asking the following questions:
	  o Do our strategies address student populations most in need of our attention?
	  o Are they likely to result in closing achievement gaps?
	  o Do they reflect knowledge of and respect for students whose culture is different than ours?
	  o Would the students and their parents in our school agree?
	  o Do any of these strategies harm or neglect any group of students or teachers?

Implementing, Monitoring, and Achieving Results	• Disaggregate student-learning data as you monitor progress toward goals. • Collect interview, survey, and/or focus group data from students from different cultures to assess the impact of implementation on them. • Make adjustments as needed in meeting the needs of students from diverse backgrounds. • Revisit the Cultural Proficiency Continuum, celebrate progress the school has made toward cultural proficiency, and set goals for further improvement. • Acknowledge individuals whose practice has become more culturally proficient. • Identify and widely disseminate practices that have been successful in closing achievement gaps.

several concrete suggestions for how to integrate attention to cultural proficiency at each stage in the Using Data Process of Collaborative Inquiry. These ideas can be a guide as well as a catalyst to your own ideas about how to bring a culturally proficient perspective to collaborative inquiry.

SUMMARY

Our assumptions and beliefs drive our interpretations of and responses to data, and culture—a predominant force in all of our lives—shapes these values and beliefs. Effective collaborative inquirers seek to understand and esteem their own culture as well as the cultures of others. They become aware of and critically examine their own assumptions and test them with additional data. Cultural proficiency—a stance of deep knowledge and respect for those whose cultures differ from ours—provides a framework and useful tools for broadening our cultural lenses and becoming more effective in educating diverse students.

As Data Teams begin to engage in conversations about data and their own assumptions, they can make use of the following tools:

- The Ladder of Inference, which illustrates how we impose our own inferences on data and even select data that reinforce our beliefs
- The Cultural Proficiency Continuum, a framework for identifying a range of responses to diversity from cultural destructiveness to cultural proficiency

By applying these ideas and tools, Data Teams can take action to strengthen their cultural proficiency at each stage of the Using Data Process of Collaborative Inquiry.

REFERENCES

Argyris, C. (1990). *Overcoming organizational defenses: Facilitating organizational learning.* Boston: Allyn & Bacon.

CampbellJones, B., & CampbellJones, F. (2002). Educating African American children: Credibility at a crossroads. *Educational Horizons, 80*(3), 133–139.

Fashola, O. S. (Ed.). (2005). *Educating African American males: Voices from the field.* Thousand Oaks, CA: Corwin Press.

Kennedy, L. (2004). *Selection criteria and student access to Algebra I.* Unpublished doctoral dissertation, Claremont Graduate School.

Lindsey, R. B., Nuri Robins, K., & Terrell, R. D. (2003). *Cultural proficiency: A manual for school leaders* (2nd ed.). Thousand Oaks, CA: Corwin Press.

Lindsey, R. B., Roberts, L. M., & CampbellJones, F. (2005). *The culturally proficient school: An implementation guide for school leaders.* Thousand Oaks, CA: Corwin Press.

Love, N., Stiles, K. E., Mundry, S., & DiRanna, K. (2008). *The data coach's guide to improving learning for all students: Unleashing the power of collaborative inquiry.* Thousand Oaks, CA: Corwin Press.

Senge, P., Cambron-McCabe, N., Lucas, T., Smith, B., Dutton, J., & Kleiner, A. (2000). *Schools that learn: A fifth discipline fieldbook for educators, parents, and everyone who cares about education.* New York: Doubleday/Currency.

Senge, P. M., Kleiner, A., Roberts, C., Ross, R. B., & Smith, B. J. (1994). *The fifth discipline fieldbook: Strategies and tools for building a learning organization.* New York: Doubleday/Currency.

Zander, R. S., & Zander, B. (2002). *The art of possibility: Transforming professional and personal life.* Boston: Harvard Business School Press.

Section 2

Stories From the Field

5 A District Uses Data to Improve Results

Johnson County, Tennessee

By Nancy Love and David Timbs

Dr. David Timbs, former supervisor of instruction for Johnson County Schools, led that district's successful implementation of the Using Data Process.

Highway 91 from Damascus to Mountain City, Tennessee, the quickest route from the Tri-City airport, twists and turns to follow the meanderings of the Laurel Creek. Ahead is a striking view of the ridges of Pond Mountain. At the easternmost point in Tennessee, early risers are treated to the first peek of the sun rising over the horizon. The signs along the way— one hand-painted "Taxidermy," another spray-painted on the side of a rundown barn exhorting passersby to vote for a local sheriff candidate—advertise the rural character of this sparsely populated, vividly green countryside. Tucked in this largely undiscovered and isolated part of Tennessee is Johnson County, where locals have lived and raised their children for generations. And nestled in the mountains of Johnson County is a school system that has much to teach the wider world about educating children.

For the last few years, effective and collaborative uses of data have catapulted the Johnson County Schools from a struggling system to one producing higher and higher student achievement levels. The county has

73 percent of its students on free-and-reduced lunch; it also has 92 percent of students in Grades 3 through 8 proficient in mathematics and 82 percent proficient in science. The school system has virtually wiped out gaps between students living in poverty and others and between students with disabilities and regular education students and scored straight As in improvement, based on Tennessee's Value-Added Assessment System results. One of the smallest and most remote schools in the county, Shady Valley Elementary, where the whole faculty acts as a Data Team, succeeded in getting every single one of its thirty-eight students, including thirteen students with disabilities, proficient in mathematics in 2006.

This chapter tells the story of how teachers and administrators in Johnson County have made this dramatic turnaround. Their case brings to life the bridge metaphor used in Chapter 1 by tracing how this small, rural school system has built the bridge between data and results. First, you will learn what achievement gains were made in Johnson County in more detail—the "results" shown in Figure 5.1. Then the case will track back to

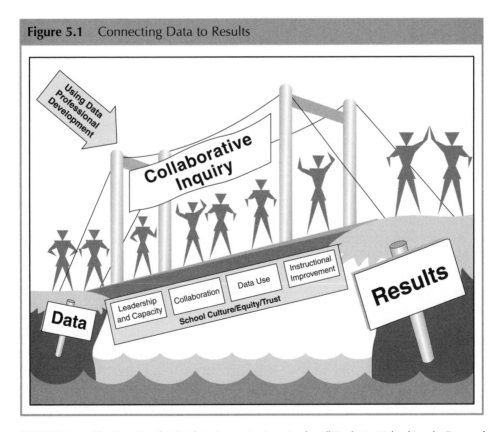

Figure 5.1   Connecting Data to Results

SOURCE: From *The Data Coach's Guide to Improving Learning for All Students: Unleashing the Power of Collaborative Inquiry* (p. 18), by N. Love, K. E. Stiles, S. Mundry, and K. DiRanna, 2008, Thousand Oaks, CA: Corwin Press. Reprinted with permission.

how the district leadership first set the conditions for successful implementation of the Using Data Process, the structured improvement process described in Chapter 3.

Next you will follow Johnson County's journey across the bridge: how leadership and capacity were built in all the schools through sustained professional development; how collaboration was established through Data Teams, which have become robust centers for collaborative inquiry; what kinds of data are used and how; and how data use has led to changes in programs, policies, and instructional practices. Finally, the authors will draw out the important lessons from Johnson County, lessons that are broadly applicable to any school system that wants to serve all of its students better, from those in the most affluent suburban schools to those in impoverished rural and urban settings.

As the leadership in Johnson County is quick to admit, what they have done is not complicated. They simply committed to the Using Data Process and stuck to it. But their message to us is powerful: dramatic and lasting improvement in student learning is possible, and neither poverty nor disabilities stand as insurmountable obstacles to high achievement.

CONTEXT

No one can minimize the challenges educators in Johnson County face. Recent U.S. Census estimates (2005) place the total population at 18,116, with almost 24 percent below the national poverty level. The annual per capita income is estimated to be $13,500, with a median household income of $24,200. Johnson County has been impacted tremendously by declining industrial jobs over the past decade, and a large percentage of the population drives to points outside Johnson County for employment. While an increasing number of retirees are moving in to take advantage of mountain vistas, pristine waters, and reasonable land prices, much of the local population continues to struggle with limited postsecondary training opportunities and a stagnant economy.

During the school year 2005–06, Johnson County Schools served 2,300 students in Grades K–12, with an additional 130 served by Head Start or by prekindergarten teachers certified in early childhood education. These students are 98 percent White, with the remaining 2 percent including small numbers African American, Hispanic, Asian, and Native American children. About three-quarters of students receive free-and-reduced lunches and about 20 percent are students with disabilities.

Historically, Johnson County schools were low performing. In 2000, Johnson County's report card issued by the state department of education was littered with Cs, Ds, and Fs. Some issues were possible misalignment among standards, curricula, and assessments; limited communication and cooperation among special and regular educators; limited parent participation; and cramped and outdated facilities. Only 38 percent of Johnson County students took advantage of postsecondary training and education.

Geographic isolation has limited students' exposure to educational opportunities. For example, the long drive to the ACT testing location, which required some students to find a ride at 5:30 in the morning, stood as a significant barrier to students' college entrance. Snow in the mountains often meant that students were missing twenty to thirty days of school in the winter. Isolation impacted teachers' professional development opportunities as well.

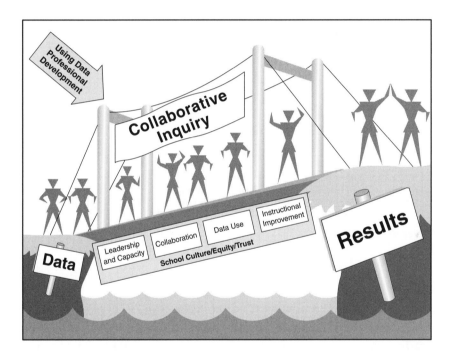

STUDENT-LEARNING GAINS IN JOHNSON COUNTY

Starting in 2003, Johnson County made a dramatic and now-sustained break with its history of low performance. Across virtually every content area and all grade levels, student performance improved from 2003 to 2006 as measured by the Tennessee State Criterion-Referenced Test (CRT) and the unique Tennessee Value-Added Assessment. Gains were made for all students, including students with disabilities and students living in poverty. For example, the percentage proficient and advanced in mathematics increased from 77 to 92 percent over three years for all students. Students with low socioeconomic status increased their performance from 72 to 89 percent. Perhaps most impressive,

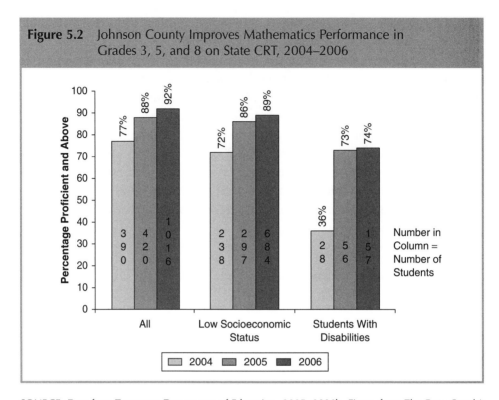

Figure 5.2 Johnson County Improves Mathematics Performance in Grades 3, 5, and 8 on State CRT, 2004–2006

SOURCE: Data from Tennessee Department of Education, 2005, 2006b. Figure from *The Data Coach's Guide to Improving Learning for All Students: Unleashing the Power of Collaborative Inquiry* (CD-ROM, Handout H1.3), by N. Love, K. E. Stiles, S. Mundry, and K. DiRanna, 2008, Thousand Oaks, CA: Corwin Press. Reprinted with permission of Corwin Press.

EDITOR'S NOTE: As we go to press, the editor has learned that student achievement gains in Johnson County evident in 2006 were sustained in 2007 (personal communication, David Timbs, May 6, 2008).

the dramatic gains for students with disabilities, from 36 percent in 2004 to 73 percent in 2005, were sustained in 2006 (see Figure 5.2).

Reading performance has also improved from 2004 to 2006 across the board—for all students, for students with low socioeconomic status, and for special education students. As in mathematics, students with disabilities made especially large gains, from 54 percent proficient in 2004 to 70 percent in 2006. Note that in 2004 and 2005, Grades 3, 5, and 8 were tested. In 2006, all students in Grades 3 through 8 were tested, which explains the big jump in the number tested that year (see Figure 5.3). Finally, science results on the Tennessee state test also improved, with the largest gains for students with disabilities (see Figure 5.4).

Not only are more students scoring proficient or above on state criterion-referenced tests, but also more students, including those on free-and-reduced lunch and those with disabilities, are moving into the advanced level, as illustrated in Table 5.1.

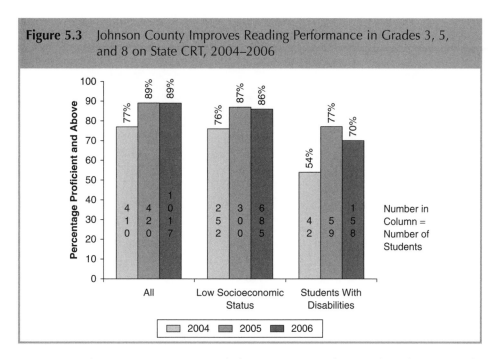

Figure 5.3 Johnson County Improves Reading Performance in Grades 3, 5, and 8 on State CRT, 2004–2006

SOURCE: Data from Tennessee Department of Education, 2005, 2006b. Figure from *The Data Coach's Guide to Improving Learning for All Students: Unleashing the Power of Collaborative Inquiry* (CD-ROM, Handout H1.3), by N. Love, K. E. Stiles, S. Mundry, and K. DiRanna, 2008, Thousand Oaks, CA: Corwin Press. Reprinted with permission of Corwin Press.

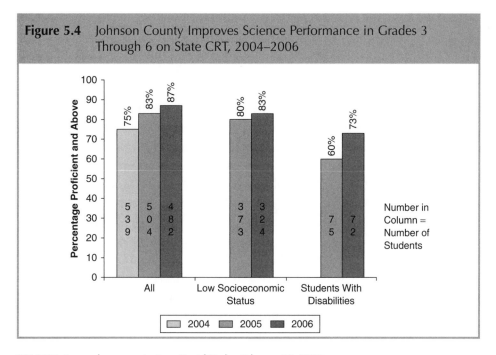

Figure 5.4 Johnson County Improves Science Performance in Grades 3 Through 6 on State CRT, 2004–2006

SOURCE: Personal communication, David Timbs, February 21, 2007.

	Percentage Advanced in Mathematics 2005	Percentage Advanced in Mathematics 2006	Percentage Advanced in Reading/ Language Arts/ Writing 2005	Percentage Advanced in Reading/ Language Arts/ Writing 2006
Table 5.1 Johnson County Increases the Percentage of Students Scoring Advanced in the Tennessee State Criterion-Referenced Test, Grades 3 Through 8, 2005–2006				
All students	32	44	30	37
Low socioeconomic status students	24	35	23	28
Students with disabilities	9	20	4	13

SOURCE: Tennessee Department of Education, 2006b.

JOHNSON COUNTY EARNS A'S FOR IMPROVEMENT

The state of Tennessee has instituted value-added assessments and been approved for their use as criteria for adequate yearly progress through No Child Left Behind. According to the state of Tennessee's grading system, Johnson County has earned straight As for improvement, exceeding the improvement rates for some of the wealthiest and highest performing districts in the state.

In Tennessee, a growth model exists to measure the growth in a student's learning from one year to the next. Developed by Dr. William Sanders, the Tennessee Value-Added Assessment System (TVAAS) sets benchmarks for gains in student scores from one grade level to the next. The model assumes that a "zero growth" in scores reflects that a student progressed through the curriculum as planned and made "one year's growth in one year's time." For example, a student whose mathematics score in fifth grade was at the 53rd NCE (normal curve equivalent, an equal interval scale that allows for comparing test scores year to year) would be expected to score at the 53rd NCE in the sixth grade, reflecting one year's worth of learning and zero growth. The state of Tennessee assigns a letter grade of C (average) on its state report card to such a score.

Johnson County School System continues to post gains much higher than the state average and has seen As in the TVAAS section of the state report card for several years in a row. This indicates that teachers are moving students much further in their learning in a year's time than is expected. In essence, they are "closing the gap" more and more in each subsequent year, resulting in higher and higher achievement scores.

Table 5.2 represents the "gain scores" and accompanying NCE scores for Johnson County in Grades 3 through 8 mathematics for 2005–06. Analysis of the chart shows that most grade levels are adding a great deal of "value" (or gain) to students' NCE scores each year. Remembering that a growth rate of 0 NCE points indicates an average expectation and earns a letter grade of C, a growth rate of greater than 1.5 NCE points indicates exemplary growth, earning a letter grade of A. The actual NCE (achievement) scores are displayed in the lower half of the table (Estimated System Mean NCE Scores).

JOHNSON COUNTY INCREASES GRADUATION AND POSTSECONDARY EDUCATION AND TRAINING RATES

State assessments are not the only measures on which Johnson County has improved. Their graduation rate has increased from 76.1 to 87.6 percent from 2003 to 2006, and the percentage of students expressing an interest postsecondary education and training has also increased from 38 percent to nearly 70 percent based on survey results of graduating high school students (personal communication, David Timbs, August 31, 2006). These and other improved results—in virtually every content area and grade level—suggest that Johnson County knows what even many high-performing schools do not: how to get better and better. The remainder of this case will examine the factors that contributed to their continuous improvement.

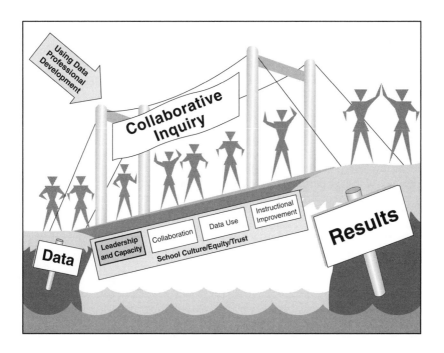

Table 5.2 2006 TVAAS System Report for Johnson County, Tennessee Comprehensive Assessment Program (TCAP) CRT Mathematics

Estimated Mean NCE Gain								
Grade:	3	4	5	6	7	8	Mean NCE Gain Over Grades Relative to	
Growth Standard:		0.0	0.0	0.0	0.0	0.0	Growth Standard	State
State 3-Yr-Avg:		1.1	2.4	1.7	1.6	1.5		
2004 Mean NCE Gain:		7.2 G	−1.8 R	1.1 G	0.6 G	−1.3R	1.2	−0.5
Std Error:		1.3	1.1	1.0	0.9	0.9	0.5	0.5
2005 Mean NCE Gain:		19.7 G	1.6 G	9.9 G	3.3 G	5.0 G	7.9	6.3
Std Error:		1.3	1.1	1.0	0.9	0.8	0.5	0.5
2006 Mean NCE Gain:		21.1G	−6.2 R*	7.5G	−1.2 R	−0.4Y	4.2	2.5
Std Error:		1.5	1.1	1.0	0.9	0.8	0.5	0.5
3-Yr-Avg NCE Gain:		16.0 G	R*	6.2 G	0.9 G	1.1 G	4.4	2.8
Std Error:		0.8	0.6	0.6	0.5	0.5	0.2	0.2

Estimated System Mean NCE Scores						
Grade:	3	4	5	6	7	8
State Base Year (1998):	50.0	50.0	50.0	50.0	50.0	50.0
State 3-Yr-Avg:	57.3	55.9	54.8	54.1	53.3	53.5
2003 Mean:	43.0	47.8	48.6	49.3	53.6	49.2
2004 Mean:	43.2	50.2	46.1	49.7	49.8	52.3
2005 Mean:	50.1	62.9	51.8	56.0	52.9	54.8
2006 Mean:	64.5	71.2	56.7	59.2	54.8	52.6

G (Green): Students made at least a year's worth of growth. The system is effective with this grade.

Y (Yellow): Students achieved somewhat less progress than expected (gain is within one standard error of the growth standard). The yellow shading provides a caution warning to the system.

R (Light red): Students in this system fell behind their peers in this grade (gain is within two standard errors of the growth standard). Light red is a stronger caution than yellow.

R* (Dark red): Students made little progress (gain is more than two standard errors below the growth standard). Dark red is the most serious of all warnings.

SOURCE: Tennessee Department of Education, 2006a.

District Leadership Sets the Conditions for Continuous Improvement

District Leadership's Conditions for Continuous Improvement

- Communicate vision clearly and often
- Align curricula, instruction, and assessment with standards
- Provide high-quality, sustained professional development for Data Teams
- Require participation of principals
- Make use of data safe and comfortable
- Provide teachers with timely access to data

The District Vision: The Little Engine That Could and What Is, Is

The first essential condition for success in Johnson County was a change of heart. The catalyst for this change was the director of schools, Minnie Miller, a native of Johnson County and former teacher and supervisor of instruction there. When Mrs. Miller was teaching at Johnson County High School, she became well known for her enthusiasm for the *Little Engine That Could* story. Whenever a student in her classroom would say he or she could not learn something, Mrs. Miller would threaten to read them *The Little Engine That Could*. The students quickly tired of "that dumb story" and trained themselves not to say or even think "I can't."

"Years later I was in a horrible accident," Mrs. Miller recounts. "I almost lost my legs and was told I would never walk again. At night I wallowed in self-pity. One day, one of my former students walked in and gave me the book *The Little Engine That Could*." After that, Mrs. Miller resolved that she was going to walk again, become the director of schools in Johnson County, and run the schools based on the-little-engine-that-could philosophy.

And that is exactly what she did. As director of schools, she asked the entire school community to board the train with her. Her can-do spirit quickly permeated the schools along with another point of view frequently communicated by Mrs. Miller and the rest of the administrative team: what is, is. The district leadership challenged teachers and administrators to put aside the things they could not affect and focus their energies on those they could. In other words, make no excuses.

Years later, when the authors of this case interviewed dozens of administrators, teachers, and students about their phenomenal success, they all pointed to these two powerful messages of "all students can learn" and "take control of what we can change" as the driving force. Even though Mrs. Miller is now retired, her philosophy has become second nature to administrators and teachers throughout the system. It is evident in the changes in data use, collaboration, instruction, student learning, and school culture that will be described below.

Special Education Is Not a Place

An important corollary of the high expectations that began to infiltrate the system was the viewpoint that "special education is not a place." What is meant by this expression is that the role of special education is to support students in learning the regular curriculum. "Special education was never meant to be a stand-alone program," explains Debra Wilcox, Johnson County's supervisor of special education. "Special education students are all teachers' students. They learn the same curriculum as regular education students. Every single child can be included."

> *Can every special education student achieve proficiency? I believe we will get mighty close.*
>
> —Debra Wilcox, supervisor of special education, Johnson County, Tennessee

The district administrative team, spurred on by Ms. Wilcox's leadership, took on the mission of enacting this throughout the system. They led an ongoing effort to do the following:

- Include special education students in the regular classroom
- Deploy special educators as consultants and partners to classroom teachers
- Spread the adaptive instructional strategies that used to occur behind closed doors in that place known as "special education" to classrooms where many more students could benefit
- Open up additional opportunities for special education students to receive assistance through tutoring programs before, during, and after school, previously reserved for regular education students
- Refine communication and coordination between special and regular educators, fully integrating special educators into every aspect of the schools, including high school departments, Data Teams, grade-level teams, and textbook selection and curriculum committees

In short, they made the commitment to stop at nothing to maximize every possible learning opportunity for students with disabilities. This vision of special education, along with that of "all students do learn, no excuses," was the backdrop to the big changes afoot in Johnson County.

Aligning Curricula, Instruction, and Assessment With Standards

One of the first ways the Johnson County Schools brought their vision to life was by embracing standards and aligning their curricula in all content areas with state standards and assessments. This effort, which began with curriculum mapping in 1999–2000, gave teeth to the commitment that all students learn by specifying what they would learn by when. It also gave teachers a clear target to aim for, so that when they began their work with data, they knew what it was they expected students to learn. Data would provide them with feedback on the extent to which students were learning the standards. The triangle in Figure 5.5 came to symbolize Johnson County's effort to "make the connections."

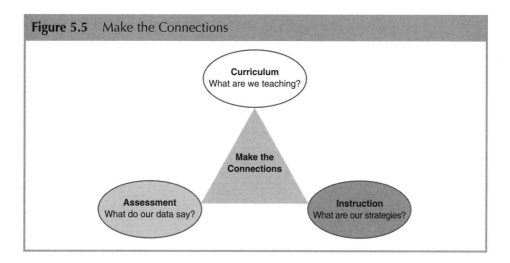

Figure 5.5 Make the Connections

Committing to Long-Term Professional Development in Using Data

Next, the system made a commitment to provide teachers and administrators with the training that they would need to use data effectively and collaboratively. It was a commitment that they considered very carefully. During the summer of 2002, several administrators and teachers in Johnson County, including the supervisor of instruction, David Timbs, attended a workshop on the Using Data approach, based on Nancy Love's book *Using Data/Getting Results: A Practical Guide for School Improvement in Mathematics and Science* (2002) and offered by the Appalachian Rural Systemic Initiative (ARSI), an initiative funded by the

> *Using Data was not an overnight process. It has taken several years for us to accomplish what we did. What started it was professional development on data.*
>
> —Gay Triplett, principal, Mountain City Elementary School, Johnson County, Tennessee

National Science Foundation (NSF) to improve mathematics and science teaching. Throughout the following year, a small group of staff experimented with disaggregated data and began to employ its use in instructional decision making.

Now the team was ready to take the next step—training Data Teams at each of the county's schools. Two ARSI staff, Terry Lashley and Colleen Wallace (now Goss), who had become Using Data Project trainers, met with the district leadership to plan training and implementation of the Using Data approach in Johnson County. Committing the time and money for six initial days of professional development workshops was a big step for Johnson County. The district leadership worried about pulling teachers out of the classroom, getting substitutes, and paying for related expenses. They seriously questioned whether their investment in time and money would pay off. The Using Data venture was a big risk for a small, rural district that had done nothing like it before, but they took the leap of faith, knowing that something had to be done to jump-start improvement in the school system.

"Get on the Using Data Train"

Just as with her little-engine-that-could message, Mrs. Miller let educators in the county know, in no uncertain terms, that they were now boarding the Using Data train. Each school put together a Data Team of teachers, special educators, and building principals and committed to the full course of professional development. Principals' participation was not optional.

Like any new initiative, Using Data met with resistance and fear. Teachers and administrators were afraid data were going to be used against them as individuals or against their schools. They were nervous about unfair comparisons being made. And they were just plain scared of data. "Most of us were horrified. One teacher had to take nerve pills. We were so intimidated by data," one Johnson County administrator confesses. "We didn't have a clue about data," another adds.

Creating a Safe Environment for Using Data

Both the district leadership and the professional developers leading the workshops took measures to make the Using Data "train ride" safe. "The workshop leaders made the environment very comfortable," explains Gay Triplett, principal of Mountain City Elementary School. From the outset, ground rules for data use were established by both the Using Data Project and the leadership in Johnson County Schools:

- Do not use data to punish individual teachers or schools.
- Do not use data as an excuse for a quick fix.
- Use data that are meaningful to teachers.
- Give teachers autonomy in responding to data.
- Look to improve practice; do not blame students or their circumstances.
- There are no secrets; we share data so we can share solutions and improve.

Principals began modeling safe data use in their own principal meeting by openly sharing their individual school data with each other. In turn, teachers learned to share their grade-level and classroom results with their colleagues. In addition, to help overcome data anxiety, the Using Data training incorporated fun and engaging ways for Data Team members to understand data. Team members created hand-drawn, newsprint-size displays of data and used a color-coding technique known as Stoplight Highlighting (Learning Point Associates, 2004; Love, Stiles, Mundry, & DiRanna, 2008). They learned a structured process of Data-Driven Dialogue and tools for getting everyone on the faculty involved and excited about data. Finally, they used highly interactive activities such as human graphs to explore concepts such as "percentile," "normal curve equivalent," and "standard deviation."

Triplett elaborates,

> The data training gave us an opportunity to be like students, to learn what the numbers mean and what to do with them. Then we did the same activities we learned in the workshop with the staff. They quickly came on board.

Data for All

Finally, the district leadership paved the way for implementation of the Using Data Process by giving all teachers access to the data that they needed. This began with Tennessee state data at every level of disaggregation possible—by school, classroom, student group, and standard. It broadened to include attendance data, graduation and postsecondary training rates, discipline referrals, and eventually, local benchmark assessment data. This democratization of data represented a huge cultural shift for Johnson County. In the past, data were available only to central office

> Data used to be held in a secure location. It did nobody any good. There was a gold mine of evidence on student achievement, and it was treated like buried treasure. We had no idea how beneficial it would be.
>
> —Teresa Cunningham, principal, Laurel Elementary School, Johnson County, Tennessee

and building administrators. Now data were in the hands of those who could use it most effectively for improvement: teachers and students.

Developing Leadership and Capacity Through an Infrastructure of Support

In many districts, the story stops after the initial training. But Johnson County was in it for the long haul. Initial workshops in the Using Data Process in 2002 were only the beginning of a four-year implementation process. Three National Science Foundation projects—the Using Data Project (UDP), ARSI, and the East Tennessee Science Partnership (ETnSP)—collaborated in Johnson County to provide coordinated and continuous training and technical assistance. The timeline in Table 5.3 illustrates the key professional development and other related activities that took place over that time period.

> We've tried different things in the past, but didn't give them time to work. Our success now has been about staying the course and working together. Now our teachers do not feel like they are out there by themselves on an island. We have all come together.
>
> —Debra Wilcox, supervisor of special education, Johnson County, Tennessee

---

Developing Leadership and Capacity Through an Infrastructure of Support

- Partner with external providers to provide ongoing professional development and onsite technical assistance and coaching over time.
- Balance pressure to participate with internal support from
  - district administrative team,
  - principals,
  - consulting teachers.

Balancing Pressure With Support

All of the training and technical assistance from three NSF-funded projects over four years would not have led to lasting change without a balance of pressure and internal support from district and building leadership in Johnson County. Mrs. Miller, director of schools, and, subsequently, her successor, Morris Woodring, asked everyone to get on and stay on the Using Data train. Each school established a Data Team. Data Teams were expected to meet regularly and implement the Using Data Process of Collaborative Inquiry and improve results for students. But the

Table 5.3 Timeline for Using Data Implementation in Johnson County

---

2002–03

- Summer 2002: Small group of administrators and teachers exposed to Using Data Process at Appalachian Rural Systemic Initiative (ARSI) Summer Institute
- 2002–03 School Year: Use of disaggregated data to make instructional decisions at system level and at some schools; planning for full implementation with ARSI professional developers

2003–04

- 2003–04 School Year: Part-time mathematics consulting teacher hired; half-time science consulting teacher (paid for and trained by ARSI) now picked up by school system; coordinated common, local benchmark assessments instituted for reading and mathematics, Grades 2 through 8, locally produced writing benchmarks for Grades K–12 (every nine weeks), and end-of-course benchmarking for Grades 9 through 12 in Algebra I, English 10, and Biology 1
- October 2003: Director of schools and supervisor of instruction commit to intensive and comprehensive training for Data Teams from each school
- November 2003: First two-day Using Data session conducted with approximately forty administrators and teachers comprising teams from every school (five elementary schools, one middle school, one high school)
- Fall–Winter 2003–04: Data Teams influence work on School Improvement Plans and prepare data-driven goals to be shared with parents, students, staff, and community
- February 2004: Second two-day Using Data session conducted

2004–05

- 2004–05 School Year: Data Team concept continues to influence decision making at the system and school level; directors of schools and administrators continue to emphasize importance of teams
- Spring 2005: Data Team concept at Johnson County High School revisited and team reconstituted to include chairs of all core departments to increase stakeholder involvement and buy-in
- June 2005: Two-day "data booster" provided by original ARSI professional developers to all Data Teams (most of whom are original Data Team members); data walls and new improvement goals created based on new data to be shared with individual staffs

2005–06

- August 2005: Data Celebration held to honor impact of Data Teams on academic improvement in Johnson County; results shared with wider audience, including officials from state Department of Education and local elected officials
- 2005–06 School Year: Data work and Data Team concept begin to be part of school system's culture; efforts shared with neighboring systems and at state and national conferences
- June 2006: Data Teams attend one-day work session to prepare data walls, share results, and set goals for 2006–07 school year

2006–07

- 2006–07 School Year: Benchmark assessments implemented in science in Grades 2 through 8 as well as in algebra, English 10, and science at high school level; Data Teams and assessment literacy are the rule and not the exception in Johnson County Schools; use of data to plan improvement at system and school level has expanded to include improvement plans that target individual classrooms and students; ongoing induction efforts train new teachers in Using Data concept as they come on board as teachers in Johnson County top-down pressure from district leadership was wisely balanced with support. The entire administrative team, all of the principals as well as consulting teachers, provided the infrastructure to support data-driven improvement.

Support From District Administrative Team

Every cause needs a champion, the point person who provides the vision as well as the constant care and feeding that a new initiative requires. In Johnson County, that champion was the supervisor of instruction, Dr. David Timbs. It was a role he was especially well suited for with his technical knowledge of data, instructional expertise, and nonthreatening and supportive approach with teachers. The director of schools delegated the leadership of the Using Data initiative to Dr. Timbs, who provided several dimensions of support that were instrumental in the implementation:

- Helped ensure that Data Teams were firmly established in each of the county's seven schools
- Met regularly with each Data Team, helping them understand the data, offering his expertise in instruction, and providing them with resources, such as instructional materials, to further their work
- Crunched the numbers and fed the teams with relevant and timely data
- Introduced benchmark assessments into the district, which became the mainstay of the team's regular data diet
- Provided considerable expertise on the use and interpretation of state test results
- Provided professional development in data use, leading the annual summer Data Day and running workshops on their benchmark assessments
- Coached new teachers in data use
- Acted as spokesperson for the County's work with other school districts and at state and national conferences

In his role as "Dr. Data," Dr. Timbs has partnered closely with Debra Wilcox, the supervisor of special education. Ms. Wilcox was instrumental in helping the Data Teams expand educational opportunities to students with disabilities and in ensuring close coordination between special and regular educators in this effort. Thanks to her leadership, every Data Team includes a special educator, and data are now widely used as a catalyst to greater inclusion of special education students in the curriculum and school program.

How a District Administrative Team Supports Continuous Improvement

- Director of schools (or superintendent) delegates the role of champion of the Using Data Process
- Champion provides constant care and feeding (e.g., meets with Data Teams and provides data, resources, professional development, and data expertise)
- Other members of the central administration (e.g., supervisor of special education) work as a team to support the initiative

The Role of the Principal

Just as every member of the district administrative team has taken on an important role in supporting the Using Data implementation, so have the principals. First, the principals throughout the system function as their own Data Team, analyzing their school results together at principal meetings. Former director of schools Miller explains, "Among the principals, everyone discussed everyone's results. We talked very openly. We weren't going to hide in the sand."

After attending all the Using Data training sessions, the principals also took on the roles of full and active participants, but not official leaders, of their school-based Data Teams. Margaret Wallace, principal of Roan Creek Elementary School, describes her role in support of the Using Data Process:

> I am a constant cheerleader. I have to demonstrate that I am willing to study our results, use research, and not make excuses. If I make excuses, the teachers will make excuses. We don't need to use data in fancy or complex ways; we just help the teachers make the best use of the common benchmark assessments and other data.

How Principals Support Continuous Improvement

- Frequently articulate high expectations, "no excuses" vision
- Cheerlead for Data Team and data use
- Actively participate as a member of the Data Team
- Delegate Data Team leadership to a teacher
- Empower teachers to make instructional decisions based on data
- Provide guidance to Data Teams around instructional interventions
- Help secure resources for Data Team and teachers, such as instructional materials
- Lead in implementing data-driven decisions, such as tutoring, parent involvement, or greater inclusion of students with special needs
- Provide time for Data Teams to meet

The Role of Consulting Teachers

The district soon realized that even this level of support was insufficient to guide a continuous improvement process. Through NSF-funded projects and other grants, the district trained consulting teachers in mathematics, science, and language arts (literacy leaders); these are teachers who were released full- or part-time from their regular teaching responsibilities to work with other teachers and students to improve teaching and learning in their respective content areas. When NSF funding ended for both the mathematics and science consulting teachers, the district continued to cover these positions through local and Title I funds. These teachers are well-schooled in data use, which they use with teachers to target their assistance to students' greatest needs.

> *I am a brushfire extinguisher. Whatever is bothering the teachers, that is what I help them with.*
>
> —Glenn James, mathematics consulting teacher, Johnson County Schools, Johnson County, Tennessee

> *At first, teachers wouldn't ask me for help. It took time to build trust. Now there are not enough hours in the day!*
>
> —Aleta Gentry, science consulting teacher, Johnson County Schools, Johnson County, Tennessee

---

How Consulting Teachers Support Continuous Improvement

- Assist in collection and analysis of data related to student learning in their content specialty
- Target assistance to teachers and students based on needs identified through data
- Conduct lessons and coach teachers in varied instructional strategies
- Provide resources for teachers (e.g., curriculum materials)
- Provide one-on-one tutoring for students who need additional help
- Facilitate teachers' learning of content in the state standards that is new for them
- Mentor new teachers

Establishing Collaboration Through Data Teams

If professional development combined with district support was the first step in building the leadership and capacity for widespread use of data in Johnson County, the second was the establishment of collaboration in Data Teams—the next step across the bridge to results. Data Teams serve as the incubator where teachers and administrators can apply and deepen

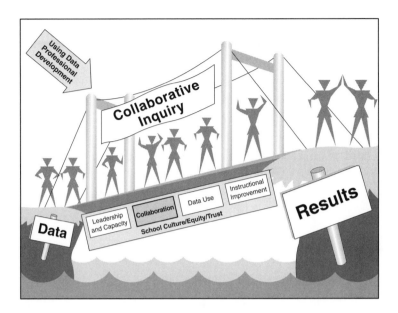

their learning about data and involve the entire school in the process. Over time, these Data Teams have acted as the catalyst to a veritable explosion of data use throughout Johnson County.

Each school in Johnson County put together a Data Team. In the elementary schools, the Data Teams include the principal, grade-level representatives, and special education teachers. Teams range in size from four to seven. In the middle school, the Data Team includes the principal and representatives from each content area and specialists. The high school Data Team includes the principal, the chair of each department, and special educators. Each Data Team has a chairperson who takes responsibility for preparing and displaying data and convening and facilitating meetings.

Both teachers and administrators have embraced Data Teams with enthusiasm. Four years after being launched, Data Teams are alive and well in all of the schools. In fact, everyone who was originally trained has remained on the Data Teams. Others have joined them.

Margaret Wallace, principal of Roan Creek Elementary School, elaborates:

> Initially, I thought I knew all I needed to know about data. I tended to take the total responsibility for data analysis on my shoulders. I didn't want my teachers to have additional responsibilities that would add to their workload. I found out through the Data Team approach how beneficial it was to expose teachers to analyzing data. It made my job easier. I don't have to do all the work. Instead, we share the responsibility for analyzing the data. It is easier and better for the teachers to say, "We've got to do this or that to increase student achievement."

Kim Kittle, Johnson County High School social studies teacher and that school's Data Team chair, agrees:

> Nothing has gotten me this excited in years. The Using Data Process in the Data Teams captivates you. It makes you realize that there is a real solution to our student achievement problems. Especially if you have taught a lot of years like I have, you can get really cynical and think it isn't going to work. Then you realize this does really work! We focused on helping all our students, and we brought everyone up. The enthusiasm is contagious.

Vignette

The Laurel Elementary School Data Team in Action

The vignette below illustrates just one of many ways that Data Teams use data to improve teaching and learning in Johnson County. In this example, the team is using individual student data from their Tennessee state assessment to provide extra help to students who need it. Notice that the team here is planning for how to help a student who is already scoring proficient on the state test do even better!

School has been in session less than a month, and already the Laurel Data Team is at work designing interventions to prevent failure and help all their students be successful. While most teachers and students are in their classrooms, members of the Laurel Elementary School Data Team are in the library grabbing their precious common planning time to examine individual students' progress on their Tennessee Value-Added Assessment results over the last three years. They are huddled around a large screen on which is projected one student's progress in mathematics.

"What happened in fourth grade?" the Data Team chair asks. "He went down by 10 percent."

"That was a really tough year for him. His parents separated and his grandma died. I know he can do better," responds another Data Team member.

"How did he do in his other subjects?" asks the supervisor of instruction, who often drops in on Data Team meetings. "Have you looked to see if this drop is isolated or shows a trend across the board? If you make some connections among the four subjects, you could possibly set some very doable goals for him. It looks like it might just take a few more questions answered correctly to get him moving back in the right direction."

It takes the team chair no time to locate the student's performance in other subject areas and observe that he was just making proficiency in social studies and science and that his language arts results had also gone down from 2005 to 2006. Just as quickly, they drill down deeper and learn what specific concepts and skills this particular student is having trouble with.

"What can we do for this child?" one team member asks. "Do you think he is a candidate for the Glow tutoring group?" The Glow group provides extra help for students who have already achieved proficiency to improve their performance even further. The school has mobilized a group of tutors, including retired teachers, their mathematics, science, and literacy consultants, and specialists. There is also a Grow group for students who have not yet achieved proficiency.

"Yes, I think so," agrees another member of the Data Team, who then offers another suggestion. "We could get some help from the mathematics consultant around instructional strategies that might work for him."

What Do Data Teams Do?

The Laurel Elementary School vignette, showing the Data Team engaged in targeting assistance to an individual student based on data analysis, provides a glimpse of just one of many activities that Data Teams engage in. While each Data Team operates slightly differently based on their context, the following are some typical functions of Data Teams in Johnson County.

Figure 5.6   A Data Team at Work

SOURCE: Courtesy of David Timbs, Johnson County Schools.

What Do Data Teams Do?

- Analyze data, take action, and monitor results
- Engage the entire faculty in using data
- Prepare data analyses and displays for use in data, cluster, and department meetings
- Identify and share best practices

Analyze Data, Take Action, and Monitor Results. This improvement cycle— analyze data, take action, and monitor results—is the meat and potatoes of the Data Team's work. Team members regularly analyze a variety of types of data, including state assessments, attendance data, and discipline referrals, using tools and processes learned through the Using Data Process, such as creating data walls to display their data (see Figure 5.7) and engaging in a structured process of Data-Driven Dialogue. At the elementary and middle school level, they drill down into Tennessee state assessment data, disaggregated by student populations and by content standard. At the high school level, graduation rates, the state's Gateway Test results,

Figure 5.7 Example of a Data Wall

SOURCE: Courtesy of David Timbs, Johnson County Schools.

ACT scores, and college and postsecondary training rates are on the table and walls at Data Team meetings. Finally, Data Teams engage in deep and frequent analysis of common benchmark assessments.

In response to all of these data, Data Teams take action:

- Initiating schoolwide programs and practices, such as refining the alignment of curricula, standards, and assessments or tutoring programs
- Improving their teaching
- Providing feedback and setting goals with individual students
- Targeting assistance to individual students

Finally, they use many of the data sources described above to monitor their progress: weekly or monthly with classroom assessment results, three times a year when benchmark assessment results come out, and annually when they receive their state test results. Each summer when these results are released, the supervisor of instruction convenes all Data Team members for a Data Day, where they examine the new data and prepare to take them back to their schools for further analysis.

Engage the Entire Faculty in Using Data. Faculty meetings are the primary venue for this. At Roan Creek Elementary School, for example, the faculty meets monthly. One month, they might look at common benchmark assessment data; another month, they examine discipline referrals. Every month, they look at attendance data because improving attendance is a schoolwide goal. The faculty brainstorms ideas. The Data Team or the administrators follow up on implementation of new ideas. The Data Team members also bring data to weekly cluster meetings in the elementary school and department meetings and engage these groups in using data as a regular part of their work.

Prepare Data Analyses and Displays for Use in Data, Cluster, and Department Teams. Often the Data Team chair will play this role. When the Data Team at Roan Creek Elementary became aware of a gender gap between boys and girls, with girls outperforming boys in both reading and mathematics, the Data Team chair began tracking gender gap data for the team. The team chair also gathered data about boys' participation in extracurricular activities compared to girls,' as they wondered if that might be a factor in the girls' higher achievement. After finding that the data showed a positive correlation between extracurricular activity and academic achievement, the team took steps to increase extracurricular participation, and boys' academic performance improved (see Table 5.6 later in the chapter).

Identify and Share Best Practices. When teachers share their data in Data Teams, something magical happens. Successful practices that were once hidden behind the classroom doors are shared. Everyone gets access to them. When data are shared in a team in a safe environment such as that created in Johnson County, they provoke conversations like this: "How did you teach nonroutine problem solving? Your kids nailed those items." "I got the kids using a graphic organizer that matched the criteria for success. That really helped." Pretty soon everyone on the Data Team is using that graphic organizer, and more and more students are benefiting from one teacher's success.

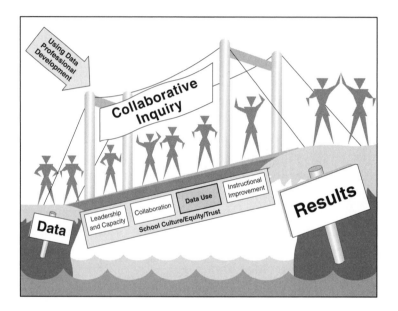

Using Data Frequently and In Depth:
Administering Common Benchmark Assessments

While Data Teams make use of a variety of data, the biggest boon to the work of Data Teams was systemwide implementation of common benchmark assessments. Beginning in 2004–05, Johnson County Schools adopted a diagnostic assessment known as the ThinkLink Predictive Assessment Series, developed through Vanderbilt University and aligned with many state tests. The Johnson County Schools also use a locally produced writing benchmark assessment for Grades K–12 and a variety of diagnostic assessments in elementary reading, including the Diagnostic Reading Assessment and the Dynamic Indicators of Basic Early Literacy Skills (DIBELS).

Valuable Features of Common Benchmark Assessments

- Aligned with state and local standards, curricula, and assessments and at varied levels of difficulty (preferably including open-response performance tasks)
- Administered at least three times per year
- Results available within a week
- Data reported by content standard, subskill, individual test item, and distractors (incorrect choices)
- All test items available for analysis
- Include open-response and performance tasks

With Data Teams and widespread data literacy already established, Johnson County teachers and administrators were poised to take full advantage of the data that was now readily accessible to them. Other districts that grab onto these tools without the professional development and structures to support their effective use can be disappointed when they do not see quick results. Leon Henley, fifth-grade teacher and Data Team member at Mountain City Elementary School, explains, "Our benchmark assessments are useless without professional development. You can't get the results without spending the time." However, in the hands of the well-primed Johnson County teachers, already organized into Data Teams, the common assessment package purchased by the district proved to be the right tool at the right time. Two sample reports used frequently by Johnson County teachers are illustrated in Figures 5.8 and 5.9.

These assessments have several features that made them immediately relevant and useful for teachers. First, they are aligned with Tennessee state standards, state performance indicators, and assessments and include questions at different levels of difficulty, from easy to moderate to hard. Second, the tests are administered three times during the school year with time in between to make improvements. Third, the results are available almost immediately—within a week—so teachers can quickly respond to them. Fourth, they give teachers the level of detail by content standard, individual test item, and individual student to know where to focus to improve their instruction. Fifth, the actual test items are available for teachers to examine. It is recommended either that common assessments include performance tasks that make student thinking visible (the assessment Johnson County purchased does not) or that Data Teams supplement multiple-choice tests with their own such items. Regardless of whether assessments are developed locally or purchased commercially, these

Figure 5.8 Predictive Assessment Series Sample Student Subskill Report: Elementary Mathematics

ThinkLink LEARNING

P.A.S. Student Subskill Report (A) School:

Discovery EDUCATION

Period: **Test 2** (20 students)
Teacher:
Class:
Grade: **3**
Subject: **Mathematics**

Blank = Correct Answer
Shaded = Incorrect Answer (student's answer shown)
"X" = Student did not answer

Subject Proficiency

Advanced
Proficient
Not Proficient
determined by # correct

Reporting Categories	Numbers/Oper					Compute					Algebra					Prob Solv					Data/Prob					Measure					Geom					Proficiency Number Correct (out of 35)	Proficiency Percent Correct	Total Number Correct
Question Number	71	72	73	74	75	41	42	43	44	45	46	47	48	49	50	51	52	53	54	55	56	57	58	59	60	61	62	63	64	65	66	67	68	69	70			
State Code	3.1.2	3.1.7	3.1.12	3.1.13	3.1.9	3.1.3	3.1.8	3.1.15	3.1.15	3.1.8	3.2.1	3.2.3	3.2.4	3.2.6	3.3.4	3.1.6	3.1.11	3.4.3	3.4.4	3.4.10	3.5.2	3.5.3	3.5.1	3.5.5	3.5.6	3.4.6	3.4.5	3.4.6	3.4.7	3.4.2	3.3.1	3.3.2	3.3.5	3.3.3	3.3.6			
Correct Answer	C	B	A	D	A	B	C	C	B	C	A	D	A	A	B	C	B	D	C	D	D	A	B	D	D	C	C	B	C	B	A	B	D	D	A			
						B	C	D			B					B		B					C	D		B	C	D	B		B	A	B	D		C		18	51%	18
							A	D			B					B	A	C			B						A	B	B	A		D		D	C		21	60%	21
	B	A	B	C		A	D	C	A	B		C			B	A	C	A	B		C	C		B		B	A	D	D			A					12	34%	12
	A	C	B	C		A	A			B		C	C	B	C	A	A	A	B	D	A		B			D			C	C						14	40%	14
		B				A	B		B		B	C	A	A		B		C	B		B			D		C										20	57%	20
	A					A	B	A	D		A	D	B			B	B	B			A		D	A			A									20	57%	20
	C					A	D			B				A			B	A	B	A																26	74%	26
			B						C		A			B				D			A															29	83%	29
							B	C			B	C		C		B									C	C										27	77%	27
	B	C				C	A			A	D			B					B						C	C										26	74%	26
	B	C				B			C		B	C		B	C		A			B	B	B														25	71%	25
	X	X	X	X	X	B	C	B	B		C	A	C	A	B	A	B	C	A	D	B	A	X	X	X	X	X									8	23%	8
					B		C	B	B		C		B	A	C	C	C																			25	71%	25
	D					B					B		B			B																				31	89%	31
	C		B	D	B	A	B	B	B	C	D	A	A	D	C	C																				20	57%	20
	B					B			B		B		D	B	C	D																				28	80%	28
	B	B		A	B	B	C	B	B	A	B		A																							24	69%	24
	B	A	C	B	D	A	C	C	A	B	C	A	C	D	C	B	A	A	D	B	C	B	D													12	34%	12
		C	D	C	A	C	B	B	A	D	A	B																								24	69%	24
	A	B	D	B	B	B	A	A	B	D	B	A																								22	63%	22

Figure 5.9 Predictive Assessment Series Objectives and Subskills Report: Elementary Mathematics

 P.A.S. Objectives and Subskills Report

School:

Period: **Test 2** (20 students)
Teacher:
Class:
Grade: **3**
Subject: **Mathematics**

Qu #	Ans	Right #	Right %	Wrong #	Wrong %	SPI	Objective Description	Reporting Category	Reporting Subcategory / Subskill	Level
								Mathematics Items		
41	B	16	80	4	20	3.1.3		Computation	3.1.3 Add, subtract single digit whole numbers	Easy
42	C	11	55	9	45	3.1.8		Computation	3.1.8 Add whole numbers to 3 digits	Mod.
43	C	13	65	7	35	3.1.15		Computation	3.1.15 Subtract whole numbers to 3 digits	Mod.
44	B	13	65	7	35	3.1.15		Computation	3.1.15 Subtract whole numbers to 3 digits	Hard
45	C	12	60	8	40	3.1.8		Computation	3.1.8 Add whole numbers to 3 digits	Mod.
46	A	10	50	10	50	3.2.1		Algebraic Thinking	3.2.1 Sort objects by 2 attributes	Mod.
47	D	19	95	1	5	3.2.3		Algebraic Thinking	3.2.3 Geometric patterns as numerical patterns	Easy
48	A	7	35	13	65	3.2.4		Algebraic Thinking	**3.2.4 One operation function rule**	Hard
49	A	15	75	5	25	3.2.6		Algebraic Thinking	3.2.6 Number/ object sorting rule	Mod.
50	B	18	90	2	10	3.3.4		Algebraic Thinking	3.3.4 Coordinates	Mod.
51	C	11	55	9	45	3.1.6		Real World Problem Solv	3.1.6 Count money	Easy
52	B	12	60	8	40	3.1.11		Real World Problem Solv	3.1.11 Money transactions	Mod.
53	D	14	70	6	30	3.4.3		Real World Problem Solv	3.4.3 Compute with calendars	Mod.
54	C	4	20	16	80	3.4.4		**Real World Problem Solv**	**3.4.4 Add/ subtract 1 or 2 digit measurements**	Hard
55	D	11	55	9	45	3.4.10		Real World Problem Solv	3.4.10 Compute elapsed time to half hour	Mod.
56	D	11	55	9	45	3.5.2		Data Analysis and Proba	3.5.2 Bar graphs	Mod.
57	A	13	65	7	35	3.5.3		Data Analysis and Proba	3.5.3 Data in tables	Mod.
58	B	9	45	11	55	3.5.1		Data Analysis and Proba	3.5.1 Pictographs	Hard
59	D	15	75	5	25	3.5.5		Data Analysis and Proba	3.5.5 Likely outcomes	Easy
60	D	12	60	8	40	3.5.6		Data Analysis and Proba	3.5.6 All possible outcomes	Mod.
61	C	11	55	9	45	3.4.6		Measurement	3.4.6 Estimate reasonable length	Mod.
62	C	4	20	16	80	3.4.5		**Measurement**	**3.4.5 Appropriate standard unit/length**	Hard
63	B	14	70	6	30	3.4.6		Measurement	3.4.6 Estimate reasonable length	Easy
64	C	13	65	7	35	3.4.7		Measurement	3.4.7 Read temperature in Fahrenheit/Celsius	Mod.
65	B	5	25	15	75	3.4.2		**Measurement**	**3.4.2 Length to centimeter or inch**	Mod.
66	A	18	90	2	10	3.3.1		Geometry	3.3.1 Two-dimensional figures	Easy
67	B	11	55	9	45	3.3.2		Geometry	3.3.2 Three-dimensional figures	Mod.
68	D	11	55	9	45	3.3.5		Geometry	3.3.5 Transformations	Hard
69	D	17	85	3	15	3.3.3		Geometry	3.3.3 Compare geometric figures	Mod.
70	A	17	85	3	15	3.3.6		Geometry	3.3.6 Line of symmetry	Mod.
71	C	16	80	4	20	3.1.2		Number Sense/Number T	3.1.2 Odd/even whole numbers	Easy
72	B	13	65	7	35	3.1.7		Number Sense/Number T	3.1.7 Compare/ order whole numbers to 9999	Mod.
73	A	10	50	10	50	3.1.12		Number Sense/Number T	3.1.12 Estimation in addition and subtraction	Mod.
74	D	11	55	9	45	3.1.13		Number Sense/Number T	3.1.13 Represent in expanded form to 10,000	Hard
75	A	15	75	5	25	3.1.9		Number Sense/Number T	3.1.9 Represent fractions with denominators to 10	Mod.

characteristics support teachers in making instructional improvements based on data.

Roan Creek Elementary School's Data Team chair, Randy Brown, explains:

> Looking at our state data was like looking into a large vat of alphabet soup and trying to read a novel. The data weren't categorized or arranged to give us enough useful information. For example, we knew our fifth- and sixth graders have had problems with measurement, but we didn't know what about measurement. We assumed measurement meant reading a ruler. We worked hard to help our students learn to use rulers, but when the state test results came back, we were frustrated by them and on the verge of state takeover. Our benchmark assessments gave us information about the specific skills within measurement that were causing our students' biggest problems and we got this information while there was time to take corrective action. It turned out that our students were not having problems reading rulers, but they were with converting one unit to another within the same system.

With detailed and timely data now readily available, Johnson County teachers quickly put benchmark assessments to work for several purposes: to refine alignment of curricula, instruction, and assessment; to improve their teaching of specific skills and address students' confusion; and to provide targeted assistance to individual students immediately—before the next assessment. Each use is described below.

Using Common Benchmark Assessments to Refine Alignment

While the district had made alignment of curricula, instruction, and assessment a priority since 2000, the use of the Predictive Assessment Series from ThinkLink has accelerated and refined this process and made it real. Teachers can now pinpoint exactly where their students' performance is weak, as in Randy Brown's measurement example above. Then they can adjust their curriculum accordingly, incorporating more time teaching and reviewing unit conversion, to continue with Brown's example.

No more pulling out of the air what to teach. We teach what the data tell us we need to teach. We've got our state performance indicator data charts on the wall.

—Aleta Gentry, science consulting teacher, Johnson County Schools, Johnson County, Tennessee

The assessments also help teachers better understand what mastery of a particular skill might look like at different levels of difficulty. If students are frequently missing application items, they adjust their curriculum to include opportunities for students to apply their skills to solving real-world problems.

Science consulting teacher Aleta Gentry offers another example:

In science, we were not teaching anything about nuclear power in sixth grade—even though it was in the standards. We've studied those standards together now, looked at various materials to use in the classroom, and are strengthening this part of our curriculum.

Drilling Down Into Common Benchmark Assessments to Improve Teaching of Specific Skills and Address Students' Confusion

When teachers drill down into their common benchmark assessments, they can discover in which specific reporting categories or strands (e.g., numbers and operations, computation) students are strong or weak. They can drill down further and learn how students performed on individual subskills within those reporting areas (e.g., estimation of place value from 100,000 to .01) and on individual test items, down to which incorrect answers (distractors) students gave. Based on all of these data, teachers can hypothesize about the source of their students' confusion and make decisions about what specific skills to teach or reteach, how to teach them (what different approaches they could use), and to whom(the whole class, groups of students, or one-on-one). Table 5.4 illustrates each of these levels of benchmark assessment data, questions to guide teachers' inquiry in each level, and responses that Johnson County teachers have implemented in their own classrooms in response to their data analysis.

Using Common Benchmark Assessments to Provide Targeted Assistance to Individual Students

Teachers also use individual student reports to finely target help for individual students. They now know each student's strengths and weaknesses in each reporting category and subskill assessed. They also know which wrong answer was given, which provides clues to the specific confusion the student might have (see Figure 5.8). Help for individual students is provided in at least three ways: by classroom and special education teachers in the classroom, by the tutoring programs available at every school, and by consulting teachers and instructional specialists. The combination of good diagnostic information and a highly developed intervention system means very few students fall through the cracks.

Table 5.4 Using Common Benchmark and State Assessment Strand-Level Data to Improve Classroom Instruction

Data Used	Questions for Inquiry	Johnson County Responses
Common grade-level benchmark assessments: Summary reports by grade level or course on percentage correct or at each proficiency level for each strand within a content area; TCAP strand data	Which standards do our students do well in? Which do they struggle with? Did we teach these standards? Did we teach them in enough detail? Did we teach them using best practices? Using strategies that reach diverse learners?	Devote more time to teaching a particular standard. Change the curriculum. Use new materials and textbooks. Stop using textbooks. Share successful strategies. Deepen teachers' content knowledge about the standard. Get assistance from instructional consultants, special educators, or building or district administrators in new ways to teach this content.
Common grade-level benchmark assessments: Reports by objectives and subskills with percentage correct for each subskill and each item within the subskill	What objectives or subskills are our students mastering? How are we teaching these? What is working? What objectives or subskills are our students struggling with? At what level of difficulty?	Share successful strategies in Data Teams and other teams. Review this subskill or objective more frequently. Teach the subskill or objective in more depth. Teach it in a different way, such as using a different modality (e.g., visual, kinesthetic). Use assistive technologies (e.g., books on tape, text-to-speech software). Deepen teachers' content knowledge around this subskill or objective. Get assistance from instructional consultants, special educators, or building or district administrators in new ways to teach this content.
Common grade-level benchmark assessments: Reports by percentage giving each incorrect answer	What patterns are we seeing around incorrect answers? Is there vocabulary our students don't understand? What confusion or misconceptions do students' incorrect responses suggest? How can we further investigate what students know and do not know (e.g., through interviews, student work)?	Share question and responses with class. Reteach directly to the confusion revealed. Analyze individual student data and target assistance.

Uses of Common Benchmark Assessments

- Refine the alignment of curricula with standards and assessments
- Identify and share best practices
- Drill down to identify specific standards that students are having trouble with and reteach, review, or teach them in a new way
- Uncover student confusion or misconceptions by analyzing wrong answers chosen and student responses to performance tasks
- Provide targeted assistance to individual students

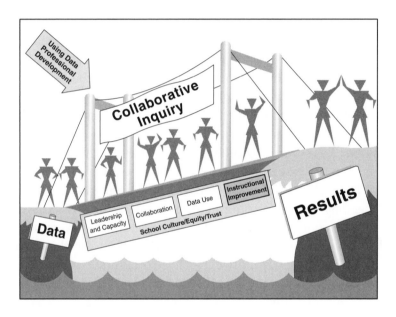

Responding to Data With Improved Practices, Programs, and Policies

Of course, it is one thing to analyze data. It is quite another to respond to data in ways that actually improve teaching and learning—the final segment of the bridge between data and results. What Johnson County has in place is a systemwide "response-ability"—the ability to respond effectively to data at the system, school, classroom, and individual student level. Driven by Data Teams that are empowered and energized to make instructional improvements, this comprehensive response system has resulted in changes to programs, classroom practices, and policies at all levels of the system, from the district office to the school, classroom, and individual student. These changes, in turn, have paved the way for the dramatic gains in student learning that Johnson County has achieved.

Changing Practices, Programs, and Policies at the District Level

Earlier in this chapter we described the ways in which the district laid the groundwork for the successful implementation of the Using Data Process by setting the expectation that all students' learning is the responsibility of everyone in the district and that special education students are part of that "all"; by committing to long-term implementation of the Using Data Process; and by mobilizing the district leadership, principals, and instructional consultants to fully support that effort.

These changes were followed by a host of others that reflect the district's ability to respond productively to data and to put into practice their can-do, stop-at-nothing approach to improving results for students. One simple but striking example is the change that was made in the school schedule. Another system might have taken the fact that it snows a lot in the mountains and that students will miss up to thirty days of school in the winter as a given. But educators and parents in Johnson County petitioned the School Board to change the calendar. Now school starts in early August so that students receive maximum instructional time before the spring assessments. This change reflects the earnest desire to let Johnson County students prove that they are as smart as students in other districts. For years, Johnson County students tested at nearly the same time as neighboring districts but with several weeks less instruction due to time missed for inclement weather. The new calendar has leveled the playing field, maximized instructional time, and boosted student confidence and teacher morale. Another example is the full integration of special and regular education so that everything, from textbook selection to training opportunities to curriculum expectations, is coordinated to maximize opportunities for students with disabilities.

Table 5.5 outlines some, but by no means all, of the ways in which the district is using data to change programs, policies, and results. Many of these changes have rippled down to the schools, which are in turn actively implementing programs and policies to improve attendance, parent participation, and student learning. The point here, though, is that responseability started at the top through the district's example and leadership.

Using Data to Improve Schoolwide Programs and Practices

The district philosophy of tackling the problems that surface in data through proactive and collaborative problem solving has taken hold in every school in Johnson County. By carrying out the functions described above, the school Data Teams lead and engage the rest of the school in using a variety of kinds of data to improve schoolwide practices, programs, and policies and provide extra help for students who need it. Table 5.6 details what one school, Roan Creek Elementary, has done in response to

Table 5.5 Using Data to Improve Practices, Programs, and Policies at the District Level

Data Used/Findings	Responses	Results
2002 Tennessee state test results: Academic achievement scores include Cs but are Ds and Fs in most core areas; Curricula are not aligned with standards or assessments; No intervention system for students who are not learning; Few teachers using data; Traditional instructional methods predominate	Commit to standards and to collective responsibility for all students' learning. Implement the Using Data Process. Establish data, cluster, grade-level, and subject-area teams; all teacher and grade-level teams meet regularly and with district leadership one day/year. Institute common benchmark assessments. Hire consulting teachers in mathematics and science and literacy leaders in Grades K–3. Coordinate special and regular education. Partner with NSF projects to improve mathematics and science education. Promote systemwide individualized assistance (e.g., tutoring, summer camps). Provide professional development in differentiated instruction and technology integration.	Continuous gains in student achievement Robust implementation of Using Data Process Data Teams functioning in every school Benchmark assessments in use to improve instruction Consulting teachers assisting teachers and individual students SMART technology in use in many classrooms Curriculum, standards, and assessments in close alignment
2004 Tennessee state test results: 36 percent of students with disabilities proficient in mathematics in Grades 3, 5, and 8 compared with 84 percent of all students; 30 percent of students with disabilities proficient in mathematics in Grades 9 through 12 compared with 84 percent of all students. 2005 Tennessee state test results: 60 percent of students with disabilities scored proficient or above in science in Grades 3 through 6 compared with 83 percent of all students (science data not available for 2004 for students with disabilities)	Spread belief that "special education is not a place." Include special education students in as much of regular education program as possible. Partner special and regular education teachers in the classroom. Increase coordination and communication between special and regular education teachers. Open all tutoring programs to special education students. Apply adaptive instructional strategies broadly in the classrooms. Use individual student data to target assistance.	In 2006, the percentage of students with disabilities proficient on Tennessee state test increased to 74 percent in Grades 3, 5, and 8 mathematics, to 58 percent in Grades 9 through 12 mathematics, and to 73 percent in Grades 3 through 6 science.

Table 5.6 Using Data to Improve Practices, Programs, and Policies at the School Level: Roan Creek Elementary School

Data Used/Findings	Responses	Results
Parent participation rate in conferences and back-to-school night less than 45 percent in 2002–03	Provide incentives for parent participation. Educate parents about their role. Improve communication. Monitor parent involvement data in faculty and Data Team meetings.	87 percent parent participation at teacher conferences in 2005–06
2003–04 Tennessee state test results (average percentage proficient across grade levels): 76 percent in mathematics, 78 percent in reading/language arts, 77 percent in science	Institute schoolwide tutoring program in "lunch bunches," before tardy bell in morning, and after school using teachers, school counselors, and mentors. Get parents on board for afterschool tutoring. Use common benchmark assessments to improve teaching. Align curriculum with standards. Institute technology application lab for Grades 5 and 6.	Every child has access to extra help as needed; More science being taught; 2005–06 Tennessee state test results (average percentage proficient across grade levels): 90 percent in mathematics, 93 percent in reading/ language arts, 88 percent in science
Comparison of data about student participation in extracurricular activities and student achievement showed that students who participate in afterschool activities have higher achievement; more girls than boys participate in extracurricular activities. Tennessee state test data in language arts and mathematics disaggregated by gender showed an achievement gap between girls and boys.	Institute campaign to increase participation in extracurricular activities, including making bus transportation available. Select more boys for student of the week and other forms of recognition. Emphasize the message to boys that "You can be successful too." Encourage boys' involvement in extracurricular activities. Provide tutoring.	Increased participation in extracurricular activities (e.g., boys' participation on student council increased by 400 percent); Increase in percentage of boys proficient in reading from 85 percent in 2005 to 95 percent in 2006; A slightly higher percentage of boys than girls are now proficient in both mathematics (4 percentage points higher) and reading (3 percentage points higher)
In 2001 and 2002, prior to opening of Roan Creek, attendance was below state and federal benchmarks at the two previous schools.	Recognize classrooms with perfect attendance in daily intercom announcement. Recognize classrooms with highest attendance each month. Monitor individual students who have attendance problems.	In 2004–05, attendance was above the state and federal benchmarks.
Discipline referrals in 2002–03: 371	Use classroom interventions. Tutor low-achieving students. Introduce counseling strategies to address multiple intelligences.	Discipline referrals in 2004–05: 297

their data and the results achieved. A similar table could easily be constructed for any of the schools in Johnson County.

Providing Extra Help for Students Who Need It

In addition to the systematic use of data to improve programs and policies at the school level, such as those illustrated in the Roan Creek example above, every school has a robust and unique system of interventions to provide extra help for students who need it. For example, Shady Valley Elementary School uses the thirty-five minutes after school when students are waiting for the bus. Instead of waiting in the bus room as they had in the past, students are now divided into classrooms every day of the week for either remedial or enrichment intervention in mathematics and language arts. Every teacher in the building volunteered to participate in the program.

Roan Creek Elementary School uses "lunch bunches," bus room tutoring, before- and afterschool study clubs, and small-group targeted assistance based on the specific needs identified in data. The vignette of the Laurel Elementary School Data Team in action earlier in this chapter showed the team examining student growth data to determine tutoring group assignments. These tutoring groups serve regular education students and students with disabilities performing at all levels—from those who have not yet reached proficiency in particular content areas to those who are proficient and moving toward advanced. The school has mobilized retired teachers, the literacy coordinator, and classroom teachers to staff the yearlong tutoring program.

> We looked at our state data at our September faculty meeting and began a discussion about what we could do to bring up our special education students' achievement. We realized that sometimes our special education students were not included in our tutoring program because we thought they were the special education teachers' responsibility. Now we focus on what all of us can do to bring our special education students up, including providing them with extra tutoring if they need it.
>
> —Margaret Wallace, principal,
> Roan Creek Elementary School,
> Johnson County, Tennessee

Using Data to Improve Classroom Instruction

While all of the changes described above, at both the district and the school level, are important, student learning does not improve unless what is taught, how it is taught, and how learning is assessed changes. Johnson County teachers are in a continual state of reinventing their teaching. Opening up ongoing dialogue about teaching based on data and sharing best practices has been

> If the horse is dead, we stop beating it and get off!
>
> —Minnie Miller, former director of schools, Johnson County, Tennessee

very productive, as supervisor of special education Debra Wilcox explains: "Teachers are willing to say, 'What I have been doing is not working.' They are changing their instruction based on data. We've given them the power to go and find out what works."

With that power, teachers have, for example, done the following:

- Studied and applied research on multiple intelligences and differentiated instruction
- Fine-tuned the alignment of their curricula with standards
- Incorporated the use of SMART boards and handheld calculators and created a technologies application laboratory, where students explore digital photography, robotics and automation, biomedical technology, and other current and career-related topics
- Studied science content together, tried out inquiry-based instruction, and accessed instructional resources from the Internet and other sources
- Incorporated the use of manipulatives in mathematics teaching
- Incorporated games and projects into their teaching
- Increased the use of writing prompts
- Adopted a new textbook that is more focused on problem solving and high-level thinking
- Expanded the use of assisted technologies for more than special education students

In fact, teachers in Johnson County have invented and implemented so many best practices that the school system organized Saturday academies, where teachers and classroom assistants teach others what they are doing that is working. They are also planning to create a Web site where teachers can systematically share their successful instructional strategies. In the early days, teachers tended to shy away from the assistance of consulting teachers; now they can't get enough of their help. As described above, much of this improvement is being driven by the common benchmark assessments; see Table 5.4 for additional information about how these data are driving instructional improvements.

Using Data With Individual Students to Set Goals and Guide Improvement

No matter how good the curriculum, how effective the teaching, and how motivated and inventive the teachers, individual students will progress at different rates and require individualized assistance. As described above,

Figure 5.10 Mystery Dot Graphs

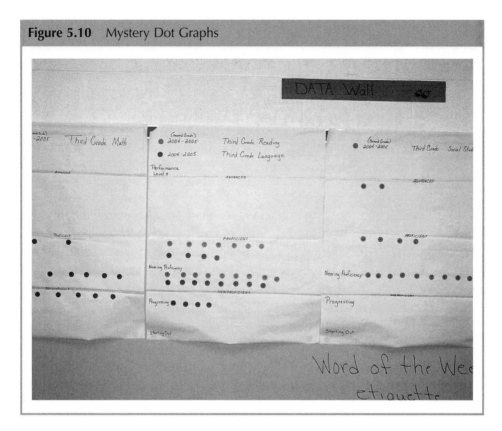

SOURCE: Courtesy of David Timbs, Johnson County Schools.

each school has devised a system for responding to individual student needs through a variety of programs. Now the Johnson County Schools are moving toward using individual test results to guide and motivate individual students to set goals and improve their performance.

Laurel Elementary School has developed its own unique approach to individual student goal-setting based on data. Go into any classroom in the school and you will find the walls adorned with what the students call "mystery dot graphs" (see Figure 5.10). These are graphs that plot the proficiency level of each individual student in the classroom for mathematics, science, and language arts using number-coded dots. Only the student and his or her parents know the secret number. These graphs have become a hallmark of parents' night at the school, when parents eagerly look for their children's mystery dots. Both the students and parents know exactly where their dot is and what the student can do to improve.

One teacher, Dianne Bauguess, who had 100 percent of her students achieve proficiency on the state test in 2006, elaborates:

> The students love how their performance is clearly visible. I had a little girl in special education. She was low in everything in second grade. She loved knowing where she was and where she needed to go. A spark was built under her. Last year, she was proficient in two areas and advanced in two. I couldn't wait to tell her. She is a different child. She actually came to me and asked, "What can I do to make straight As?"

This year Laurel took the mystery dot idea a step further. Each student now has an individual conference with his or her teacher, where they discuss the student's individual test results on a variety of measures and set very specific targets for improvement. Then they discuss what the student can do to meet those targets. Devised by a special education teacher on the Data Team, this process makes the benefits of an individualized education plan available to every student. "I have to bring myself up in math," one Laurel student enthusiastically declared. When asked how he was going to achieve that, he replied without hesitation, "I need to listen better in class, work on graphing, and do my homework."

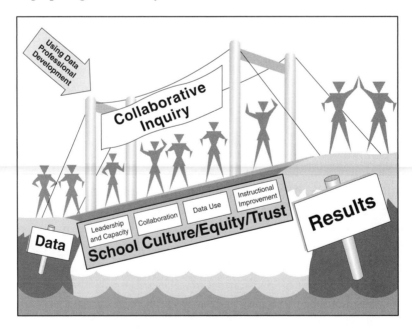

Culture Change: The Foundation of the Bridge

Today a visitor doesn't have to look hard to find evidence of the strong presence of data use throughout Johnson County. Data are as regular a part of the school day for administrators, teachers, and students as school buses,

Figure 5.11 Data Wall at a Johnson County School

SOURCE: Courtesy of David Timbs, Johnson County Schools.

class schedules, white boards, and books. When you walk into most schools, for example, you will see data walls displaying their current Tennessee state test results posted in the lobby (see Figure 5.11). Data show up on the walls of faculty rooms; at most faculty, cluster, department, and principal meetings; staff development sessions; parent nights; and in many classrooms.

Four years after Johnson County's first exposure to the Using Data Process, Using Data is no longer an initiative in Johnson County; it is a regular practice, the way things are done. This is because leadership of the Using Data Process is now widespread and institutionalized throughout the schools in high-performing Data Teams. Virtually every teacher has become an expert in the types of data they use to improve their instruction. Most cannot imagine doing their job without data and without each other. New teachers are quickly inducted into the process. What is emerging is capacity—"the collective ability," as Michael Fullan (2005) defines it, "to act together to bring about positive change" (p. 4).

When you ask educators in Johnson County what's next, they have a long list: move more students to advanced levels of performance; improve writing across the system; revitalize the high school Data Teams; further improve the performance of students with disabilities; incorporate more rigor into the curricula, going beyond the expectations of the Tennessee state standards; expand use of formative and performance assessments.

Continuous improvement has become a habit, one that is supported by line items in the budget for common assessment data, structures for collaboration, widespread data literacy, and belief in the capacity of every student to achieve—no excuses. Not only have the Johnson County Schools overcome their geographic isolation to open up more educational opportunities for students and teachers, they have built a strong bridge between data and results, one that we suspect will withstand the test of time.

Lessons Learned

The lessons learned in Johnson County are not unique to this small rural school system. They can be generalized to any school system with room for improvement.

Lessons Learned

- District leadership sets the conditions for change.
- If there is not a coordinated effort to sustain change from the district leadership to building principals to teachers, the change will not take root.
- Systemic change is only a phrase until changes are made and stuck with for at least two to three years.
- Beliefs about students and their capabilities are the driving force behind culture change.
- Professional development in data literacy, improvement processes, and effective instruction is critical to improving student performance.
- It is through teacher collaboration that effective uses of data to improve instruction occur.
- Data only tell us what is going on, not what to do; responses to data rely on understanding both data and research, content being taught, and best practices.
- Data, including regularly administered common assessments, must be made widely available and shared in a safe environment.
- Common assessments analyzed at the item and subskill level provide rich information for improving instruction.
- Maximum inclusion of special education students and a collaborative effort on behalf of all students can dramatically reduce achievement gaps.
- Success breeds success, and celebrations that acknowledge and spread successful practices provide momentum for continuous improvement.

REFERENCES

Fullan, M. (2005). *Leadership and sustainability: System thinkers in action.* Thousand Oaks, CA: Corwin Press.

Learning Point Associates. (2004). *The toolbelt: A collection of data-driven decision-making tools for educators.* Naperville, IL: Author.

Love, N. (2002). *Using data/getting results: A practical guide for school improvement in mathematics and science.* Norwood, MA: Christopher-Gordon.

Love, N., Stiles, K. E., Mundry, S., & DiRanna, K. (2008). *The data coach's guide to improving learning for all students: Unleashing the power of collaborative inquiry.* Thousand Oaks, CA: Corwin Press.

Tennessee Department of Education. (2005). *Johnson County report card 2005.* Retrieved October 1, 2007, from http://www.k-12.state.tn.us/rptcrd05/system2.asp?S=460

Tennessee Department of Education. (2006a). *2006 TVAAS system report for Johnson County, TCAP CRT math.* Retrieved February 14, 2007, from http://tvaas.sas.com/evaas/Reports/TVAAS_DistVA.jsp?districtid=460

Tennessee Department of Education. (2006b). *Johnson County report card 2006.* Retrieved October 1, 2007, from http://www.k-12.state.tn.us/rptcrd06/system2.asp?S=460

6

A Data Team Problem Solves About Problem Solving

Clark County, Nevada

By Lori Fulton, Thelma Davis, Janet Dukes,
Greg Gusmerotti, and Joan Lombard

Lori Fulton was formerly Super Data Coach and project facilitator for mathematics, science, and technology in the Clark County School District; Thelma Davis was coordinator of K–5 mathematics and science, Clark County School District; Janet Dukes and Greg Gusmerotti are teachers and Data Coaches at Katz Elementary School; and Joan Lombard is principal of Katz Elementary School.

This is the story of how collaborative inquiry unfolded in one elementary school within the large urban district of Clark County, Nevada, a Using Data Project pilot site. Participating staff tell how each stage of the Using Data Process played out in the Katz Elementary School, including commentary from the principal and the project facilitator.

Based on material from *The Data Coach's Guide to Improving Learning for All Students: Unleashing the Power of Collaborative Inquiry* (2008) by Nancy Love, Katherine E. Stiles, Susan Mundry, and Kathryn DiRanna. Adapted with permission from Corwin Press.

BUILDING THE FOUNDATION

Located in the northwest region of the Clark County School District, the Katz Elementary School serves approximately 800 students in Grades K–5. The school is mixed ethnically with 48 percent White, 23 percent Hispanic, 20 percent African American, 8 percent Asian, and 1 percent Native American. Ten percent of students are limited English proficient and 42 percent qualify for free-and-reduced lunch.

After learning about the Using Data Project in the spring of 2003, the school staff formed a Data Team focused on mathematics improvement. The team initially consisted of four Data Coaches including the new principal, one primary-level and one intermediate-level teacher, and a district-based project facilitator who provided assistance to the school in the areas of mathematics and science.

Establishing the Data Team

As the Data Team prepared to meet, the Data Coaches talked with individuals at each grade level to encourage them to join the work, explaining the potential benefits for the students. Little did the team know how important this move was to building a strong foundation for their work. The invitation resulted in increased diversity and depth on the Data Team, which now consisted of ten people: one representative from each grade level, K–5, one primary site-based Data Coach, one intermediate site-based Data Coach, the school's new principal, and the district-based project facilitator.

The principal saw the potential the Data Team had to influence professional development, collaboration, and student learning throughout the school and wanted to capitalize on that potential by preparing the way for a strong, collaborative team. The new Data Team established a schedule to meet after school every other week in the school library for ninety minutes. The principal made these meetings a priority and attended every one as a fellow Data Coach. The other Data Coaches worked as a group to introduce the Data Team members to the collaborative inquiry process. During these initial meetings, they utilized data from the previous year's Iowa Test of Basic Skills to introduce members to the tools from the Using Data Toolkit.

The new team began to take root. Since there was now representation from all grade levels on the Data Team, the team had a mechanism to actively involve the entire faculty. During the Data Team meetings members examined schoolwide data, enabling the team to develop a more comprehensive view of school practices and results and to discover the importance of understanding how learning develops across the grade levels. Team members took responsibility for communicating Data Team observations, findings, and ideas to all faculty members at the monthly grade-level meetings. This created an opportunity to gather input and develop ideas further.

While this was a good start, the Data Coaches soon realized that this structure would fall flat if they did not do something to acknowledge and support the change in school culture that the Using Data Process was promoting. Therefore, they decided to bring all staff members together and to work as a group to establish a schoolwide culture of collaborative inquiry around data. The Data Team knew that this culture would be key to ensuring that the new grade-level-based structure was successful in involving all staff members in the process.

Involving the Whole Faculty

Accordingly, the team began to engage faculty from all grade levels in learning more about data. They explored who their students and teachers were demographically, what they wanted to learn from the data, and the positive aspects of their school and challenges to be met.

Katz operates on a five-track, year-round schedule. The school year begins in August and ends the following August. There are staggered breaks throughout the year, and one-fifth of the students and staff are on break at all times. Each track contains at least one classroom for each grade level K–5. At the faculty's first meeting with the Data Team, each track shared with the entire group a picture of their data and what the staff members were thinking about critical aspects of the school.

Two months later, the Data Team brought the staff together again to strengthen understanding of the shifts in culture the school hoped to make and to develop a commitment to working collaboratively to improve the school. The Data Team created a fun-filled day with activities that helped establish unity and a sense of teamwork and drove home the message that everyone, not just the Data Team, was a part of the data project and would play a role in the mission to improve the school.

Finally, the staff dug into student data. Using data from the mathematics portion of the state's criterion-referenced test (CRT), the Data Team broke staff into grade-level groups. First, they made predictions of what they thought they would see when they looked at the data. Then, using predetermined cut-points based on district and school standards, the grade-level groups painted a picture of student achievement. Next, the groups went on to observe the data, make inferences, and display their data for all to see. The staff ended the day by looking for and noting trends using this one piece of data. As a next step, the Data Team decided that it would build on this data analysis by digging deeper into state CRT and other data to identify a student-learning problem.

Project Facilitator's Commentary

As an outside member of the Data Team, I think the transition that took place with this school was a healthy one. The new principal's emphasis on collaboration and shared decision making caused the team and, ultimately, the school to back up and reestablish their beliefs about collaboration. . . . The commitment displayed by the principal played a key role in the success of the Data Team and the school. She was present at all meetings and served as a side-by-side leader, learning and making decisions with the team rather than on her own. Furthermore, the structure of the team and their dedication to building a strong foundation to work from helped establish a culture of collaborative inquiry within the school.

Principal's Commentary

As a new principal in the building, I wanted to get to know the staff and what they considered to be important. I knew they had gone through quite a bit of change over the past few years and that the last two administrators had had very different styles. I knew that one of the first tasks we needed to do was rebuild the community within the school. The data gave us a reason to have a discussion and begin to examine who we are as a school. I knew the Data Team could play an important role, and I saw it as more of a steering committee for the entire school rather than a group of isolated people. If this was to be the case, though, I felt very strongly that the Data Team needed to grow to include representation from all grade levels.

IDENTIFYING A STUDENT-LEARNING PROBLEM

In order to get a clear picture of what was happening in the mathematics curriculum at Katz Elementary School, the Data Team decided to focus on three sources of data: the state criterion-referenced test, given in Grades 3 and 5; the norm-referenced test used by the district, the Iowa Test of Basic Skills (ITBS), given in Grades 3, 4, and 5; and an open-response test utilized by the school and the district, the Mathematics Assessment Resource Services (MARS) assessments, given in Grades 3, 4, and 5. The team first decided to examine the MARS assessments, which usually consist of four to five tasks, each with either a single problem or a sequence of problems. Together these tasks allow students to demonstrate their mathematical ability in both content and processes outlined in the National Council of Teachers of Mathematics (NCTM) Standards. Selected schools in Clark County administer these assessments in the fall and then send them in to be scored by a trained team.

When Katz Elementary School received the results for the MARS assessments, the Data Team brought all third-, fourth-, and fifth-grade teachers together to look at the data using the tools of the Using Data Process. Substitutes were provided for the teachers so they could attend the professional development session. Grade-level groups worked independently to make predictions, create visual charts, make observations, and finally make inferences about the data. This information was then shared with the other grade-level groups. Once all groups had examined the aggregated data, they began to look at how students performed on each of the five tasks on the assessment. Figure 6.1 illustrates the percentage correct on each of the five third-grade tasks.

Then they drilled down further into the results for each question or item within the multiquestion tasks. Examining these data from Grade 3 to Grade 5 brought about a lively discussion and a recognition that student performance declined as students progressed through the years. They formulated inferences about the data, which included the following:

- Test items became more difficult in Grade 5 and were much more reading-intensive.
- Students' stamina gave out by the end of the test, resulting in lower scores on later problems.
- Students were not exposed to these types of problems on a regular basis.

The team decided to look at the ITBS results next. They predicted what they would see in the third-, fourth-, and fifth-grade data. They created a visual picture of the strengths and weaknesses of their students' performance in mathematics, made observations based on the data, and then discussed inferences and questions about the data. This process was completed for all grade levels as well as across the three grades.

Finally, the Data Team looked at a third source of data, third- and fifth-grade mathematics results from the 2002–03 state criterion-referenced test. Starting with aggregated data, they observed that 60 percent of third

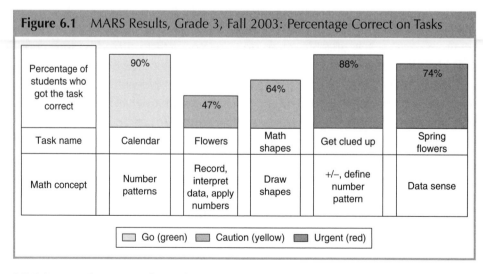

Figure 6.1   MARS Results, Grade 3, Fall 2003: Percentage Correct on Tasks

Percentage of students who got the task correct	90%		64%	88%	74%
		47%			
Task name	Calendar	Flowers	Math shapes	Get clued up	Spring flowers
Math concept	Number patterns	Record, interpret data, apply numbers	Draw shapes	+/–, define number pattern	Data sense

☐ Go (green)   ☐ Caution (yellow)   ■ Urgent (red)

SOURCE: From *The Data Coach's Guide to Improving Learning for All Students: Unleashing the Power of Collaborative Inquiry* (p. 343), by N. Love, K. E. Stiles, S. Mundry, and K. DiRanna, 2008, Thousand Oaks, CA: Corwin Press. Reprinted with permission.

graders were proficient or above compared to 52 percent of fifth graders, the same pattern of decreasing performance from Grade 3 to Grade 5 was observed in the MARS data. Their analysis of disaggregated data revealed that the gap between White students and African American and Hispanic students was wider in Grade 5 than in Grade 3. Then they examined their strand-level data, illustrated in Figure 6.2.

Based on all the data examined, the teachers then made a series of observations and inferences and were ready to identify a student-learning problem. Examining all the data together, the team noted that problem solving by fifth graders was a common area of concern in all three sources. Since they had also identified this as an area of concern when looking at the pre-CRT data, they felt that this was the student-learning problem that should be focused on first. They crafted the following problem statement:

- Fifth-grade students are below acceptable levels in problem solving.
- Fifth graders scored below proficiency with an average of 51 percent correct in problem solving as evidenced by performance on the 2002–03 CRT.
- Sixty-one percent of fifth graders are below proficiency in problem solving as evidenced by performance on the 2003–04 pre-CRT administered in December 2003.
- Eighty-nine percent of a sample of fifty-six fifth graders scored below acceptable proficiency on MARS problem-solving assessments administered in December 2003.

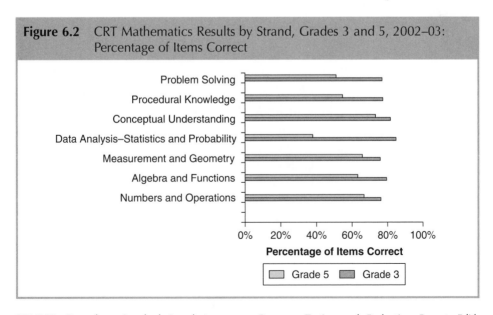

Figure 6.2 CRT Mathematics Results by Strand, Grades 3 and 5, 2002–03: Percentage of Items Correct

SOURCE: Data from Standards-Based Assessment Program, Testing and Evaluation Report, Edith and Lloyd Katz Elementary School, 2002–03. Figure from *The Data Coach's Guide to Improving Learning for All Students: Unleashing the Power of Collaborative Inquiry* (p. 344), by N. Love, K. E. Stiles, S. Mundry, and K. DiRanna, 2008, Thousand Oaks, CA: Corwin Press. Reprinted with permission of Corwin Press.

Throughout this stage, the Data Team recognized the importance of involving the entire staff in the process. The team provided the staff with regular updates in staff meetings and posted charts in the staff lounge for everyone to see. This allowed the entire staff to stay on top of what was happening without requiring that everyone be equally involved.

Project Facilitator's Commentary

The process of drilling down into multiple pieces of data takes a great deal of time—something most teachers and administrators don't feel that they have. Throughout the process, it seemed as though I needed to be a cheerleader and remind the group that the work they were doing was important and part of a bigger picture. Since we get caught up in issues of time and want to fix things right away, we often jump to making inferences based on tiny pieces of data. A major role for me throughout this process was to help clarify the difference between an observation and an inference and to remind people where we were in the stages of Data-Driven Dialogue, reminding them that inferences need to be examined and checked out to help us take the best actions. I think the idea of predictions also played an important part but was sometimes left out. As we make predictions, we are stating our own assumptions and biases. Unless we put them out on the table and then take the time to really observe what we see before us, these biases can influence the decisions we make without our realizing it. As we worked through the dialogue process, I would often hear teachers express amazement at the difference between what they thought they would see and what they actually saw. To me, this was a major learning. It helped us see beyond what we normally see and bring about change.

Principal's Commentary

We learned so much through this process. First, the visual representation and color-coding using Stoplight Highlighting was quite an eye-opener. Seeing the data displayed visually with so much red (urgent) and yellow (caution) really made us want to dig further for a better understanding. The amount of time it took to drill down was frustrating, yet as we went through the triangulation process with our data sources, we experienced many "aha's." We realized that the data we had available to us did not always allow us to go as far as we wanted to. We decided that we needed other assessments put in place that we could use to examine data at the item level, something we were unable to do with the CRTs and the Iowa Test. This caused us to create our own benchmark assessments in mathematics so we would have them as future data resources. Overall, this was an eye-opening experience for us as a school.

Verifying Causes

With the problem statement now firm in everyone's mind, the Data Team needed to determine causes that might be leading to that problem. For this they used the Fishbone, a graphic organizer for brainstorming multiple causes of a problem, and generated the possible causes shown in Figure 6.3.

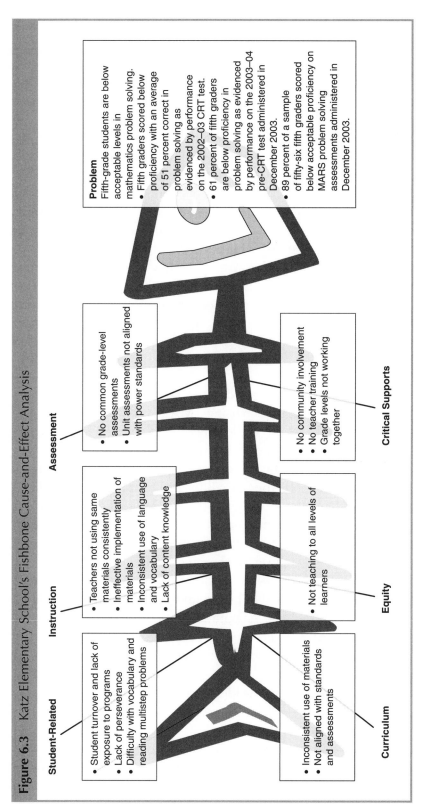

Figure 6.3 Katz Elementary School's Fishbone Cause-and-Effect Analysis

Student-Related
- Student turnover and lack of exposure to programs
- Lack of perseverance
- Difficulty with vocabulary and reading multistep problems

Instruction
- Teachers not using same materials consistently
- Ineffective implementation of materials
- Inconsistent use of language and vocabulary
- Lack of content knowledge

Assessment
- No common grade-level assessments
- Unit assessments not aligned with power standards

Problem
Fifth-grade students are below acceptable levels in mathematics problem solving.
- Fifth graders scored below proficiency with an average of 51 percent correct in problem solving as evidenced by performance on the 2002–03 CRT test.
- 61 percent of fifth graders are below proficiency in problem solving as evidenced by performance on the 2003–04 pre-CRT test administered in December 2003.
- 89 percent of a sample of fifty-six fifth graders scored below acceptable proficiency on MARS problem solving assessments administered in December 2003.

Curriculum
- Inconsistent use of materials
- Not aligned with standards and assessments

Equity
- Not teaching to all levels of learners

Critical Supports
- No community involvement
- No teacher training
- Grade levels not working together

SOURCE: From *The Data Coach's Guide to Improving Learning for All Students: Unleashing the Power of Collaborative Inquiry* (p. 347), by N. Love, K. E. Stiles, S. Mundry, and K. DiRanna, 2008, Thousand Oaks, CA: Corwin Press. Reprinted with permission.

Then, applying Spend-a-Buck, a simple prioritizing strategy, the Data Team used colored dots to mark areas they felt were contributing most to the student-learning problem. Each member was provided with four dots to "spend" to indicate the causes of the problem. After all members had placed their dots, the team tallied the results and considered which cause they would look into further.

The results indicated that the team believed the problem was student related. The possible causes that received the highest votes were lack of strategies, lack of perseverance, and lack of reading skills. Based on the data, the team decided to look further into perseverance as the cause of the problem. They felt that a strong piece of evidence to support this cause came from the MARS data: students had consistently done worse on problems that occurred later in the test. This led the Data Team to two conclusions. First, they felt that students grew tired as they went through the test and lacked the perseverance to finish it. Second, they thought that students did well on the beginning portion of a problem but were not persisting within the problem, causing them to do poorly overall.

Examining Student Work

To test their possible cause, the team devised a plan to test forty randomly selected students in Grades 3 through 5 using a MARS task, "Addworm." The team decided to have the students complete this task in an interview-style format, where a teacher would watch and take notes as students worked through the problem (see Appendix A at the end of this chapter for an illustration of a student's work on this task and Appendix B for an illustration of a teacher's observations of a student working on the task). This would allow the teachers to assess the extent to which students persevered through the task or gave up early. They also decided to provide multilink cubes as manipulatives for students to use on the task if they chose to. The cubes would be available on the table, but the facilitating teacher would neither encourage nor discourage their use. All team members agreed to help with the task and the interviews, working with students during their preparation periods or administering the task during their track breaks. To ensure that everyone administered the task in the same manner, they created a script for teachers to follow.

After six weeks of working with students, the team had managed to complete the process with a majority of the identified students, so team members shared the data they had gathered and the observations they had made:

- Students were willing to struggle with the problem for an extended period of time and did not give up on the task as had been proposed.
- Students seemed to understand the task, as evidenced by their responses to the interview questions.

- Students seemed to lack a variety of strategies for solving the problem and attempted to solve the problem in a similar manner; very few drew pictures to represent their thinking or made use of the manipulatives provided.
- Students who did use the manipulatives or had a variety of strategies tended to come from classrooms that relied heavily on one of the school's mathematics curriculum materials, Investigations in Number, Data, and Space.

The information the team now had before them indicated that perseverance and reading comprehension were not the causes of the low scores in problem solving as they had initially thought, but that the problem might be more directly tied to the instruction and the types of tasks teachers were using with students. The fact that students did not make use of the manipulatives and struggled to come up with strategies for solving the task led the team to believe that students were not being exposed to a variety of strategies on a regular basis in the classroom. A team member also suggested that an upcoming change in staff would present a new challenge, in that several of the incoming staff had probably not received training in full implementation of the school's curriculum, nor would they have experience with use of the pedagogy the school was attempting to use, including inquiry-based learning and higher-level questioning. The team found research to support the idea that students learn when presented with a coherent curriculum and that teachers' understanding of pedagogy and content influences student learning. With this information in hand, the team decided to investigate instruction and effective implementation of the school's mathematics curriculum as possible causes to verify with local data.

The next step was to share with the staff where they were in the process. At the next staff meeting, the team presented the data they had collected during the student interviews and the conclusions they had drawn. Next, the team explained the research on curriculum implementation and its relationship to student learning and made the case for now pursuing instruction as a possible cause of the student-learning problem.

Collecting Local Data About Curriculum Implementation

The team felt that it was important to explore further this idea of a coherent curriculum and enlisted the help of the principal to gather data. It was determined that old lesson plans might provide evidence of the type of mathematics instruction taking place in the classrooms. As a next step the principal agreed to review teachers' lesson plans covering a two-week time span to determine how many lessons were based on the use of the school's curriculum materials. Over the next week, the principal scanned lesson plans for nineteen teachers and found that seventeen indicated a consistent use of the curriculum over the two-week period. The other two sets of lesson plans did not have any indication that the district's curriculum materials were being used.

During this time period the principal also conducted classroom "walk-throughs" to see what type of instruction was taking place during the mathematics period. These visits demonstrated that although most teachers had stated in their lesson plans that they intended to use the curriculum materials and strategies, this was not always evident in practice. Moreover, when the principal did see evidence of the curriculum being implemented, she noted that it was being taught in a very mechanical manner and that the questions being posed were often at the lower level of Bloom's taxonomy (Bloom, 1984). The principal also noted that teachers were supplementing with various materials that lacked the higher-level thinking skills the team thought should be in place.

These data along with the research the team studied served to verify two causes of the student-learning problem:

- Teachers do not expose students to higher-level questions on a regular basis.
- Teachers are not implementing the mathematics curriculum in a consistent manner.

Project Facilitator's Commentary

While this proved to be a frustrating time for the group, I think it was some of the most valuable time spent. The team dug into the "verify cause" process and found that if they had followed their first instincts, they would have ventured down the wrong path. I think the group's first inclination to identify the problem as student related is very natural. It is easier to put the burden on students rather than examine our own practices more closely. Because the team chose to study the issue in more depth, however, they gained valuable information that they were able to use to move forward. The verification process proved to be a valuable learning experience, as it demonstrated the need for ensuring that a problem really exists before throwing money and time at it in order to make it better.

Principal's Commentary

We had ideas of what was leading to students' low problem-solving scores, but the issue of problem solving seemed so big that we did not know where to begin or what type of assessment to use to analyze it further before moving into solutions. When the team came up with the idea of using a common assessment in a one-on-one interview style, I thought that was a good idea. It proved to be very eye-opening, as it steered us down a different path than we were on. Even though this task was very time-consuming, I think it empowered the teachers because they became so well informed of the issues that lay before us. It led us to a more valid conclusion due to the effort that was put forth during this stage of the Using Data Process.

Generating Solutions

Once the team had verified a likely cause for the student-learning problem, they moved on to seek valid solutions to the problem. Working through the Using Data Logic Model, a graphic organizer illustrating the logical sequence from strategies to results, they listed the causes and generated strategies to address the causes, specified the outcomes they expected from implementing the strategies, and developed a plan for monitoring the outcomes. The team's Logic Model is shown in Figure 6.4.

While generating solutions, the team drew upon the expertise of the group members and the many years of training they had through the Mathematics and Science Enhancement (MASE) Project. The team searched for articles on questioning and found resources for the teachers about Bloom's taxonomy, and they provided each teacher with an easy reference card with examples of the different levels of questioning that could be used during planning and lessons.

Like the Verifying Causes phase of the Using Data Process, this final phase was a difficult process for the team. They knew what they hoped to accomplish, but deciding how to implement the plan proved to be difficult. Once the strategies were determined, the team had to grapple with the problem of how to monitor progress along the way. This particular stage seems to have been a bit weaker than others simply because the team wasn't used to thinking about monitoring progress over the long term. They were more accustomed to applying a quick fix to a problem in order to see test scores rise in the next round and then move on to the next crisis. The Using Data Process challenged the team to think and act differently by constructing and implementing a longer-term action plan directly tied to a particular student-learning problem.

Project Facilitator's Commentary

Although I have worked with schools for years to address the needs of professional development, I had a difficult time with this stage and felt unprepared to help the team move forward. Although the Logic Model made perfect sense and was something I should have been using for years, it was new to me and I struggled to make sense of all the parts and pieces. To help with this learning process, I decided to apply the Logic Model to some of my own work. Rather than going it alone with this tool, I enlisted the help of the Using Data Project staff and my colleagues at the Data Team meeting where we planned to put our own Logic Model together. The idea of actually monitoring our progress was novel. For the past few years, we had offered a variety of professional development opportunities to the teachers. The sessions were worthwhile and provided assistance to teachers with what we thought were problems within the school. However, we never actually monitored the impact of the professional development to find out whether

Figure 6.4 Katz Elementary School's Logic Model

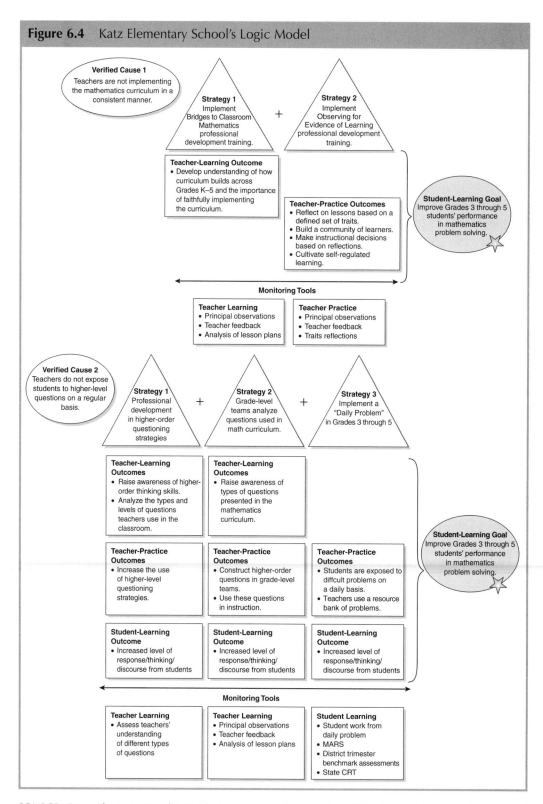

SOURCE: From *The Data Coach's Guide to Improving Learning for All Students: Unleashing the Power of Collaborative Inquiry* (pp. 352–353), by N. Love, K. E. Stiles, S. Mundry, and K. DiRanna, 2008, Thousand Oaks, CA: Corwin Press. Reprinted with permission.

progress was really taking place. I think we learned a great deal about generating solutions during this stage, but monitoring implementation and impact is something the team will need to continue to develop its capacity to do in our school.

Principal's Commentary

We are still in this stage. We are learning how to use Bloom's taxonomy in order to bump up our level of questioning. We have examined the questions presented in our math curriculum and found a stronger relationship between the types of questions presented in Investigations in Number, Data, and Space and on the criterion-referenced test. We did this correlation as an entire staff and it generated a great deal of dialogue. In doing this, we also found that the types of questions asked in Investigations in Number, Data, and Space are inductive. This most likely presents an issue for those students who are deductive learners and for the teachers in making connections for those students.

TAKING ACTION AND CELEBRATING RESULTS

In the fall of 2004, the team hit the ground running, ready to implement strategies to improve student learning. A team of K–5 teachers was selected to learn about a modified version of the popular lesson study model, Observing for Evidence of Learning (OEL), which would serve as a valuable tool for focusing on lessons and the level of questioning that was involved. This team returned to the school to facilitate grade-level meetings in which teachers worked together to plan a lesson in mathematics, implement the lesson, and then debrief the lesson. Teachers found this to be a useful process for focusing on the essential components of a lesson: the mathematical content, instructional practices, and questioning strategies.

Meanwhile, another group of teacher–leaders facilitated professional development on the Bridges to Classroom Mathematics curriculum. All teachers were scheduled to attend five three-hour sessions designed to help them understand how concepts from Investigations in Number, Data, and Space built on one another. Participants were to learn how concepts were developed and practiced within this curriculum and the importance of implementing such components as choice time, games, and 10-minute math. It was hoped that this professional development would help teachers begin to understand the importance of implementing the curriculum fully to allow students time to develop concepts at different levels each year. Teachers attended their first session in October, and the feedback indicated that it had the potential of being a useful monitoring tool, as teachers expressed amazement at seeing how a concept they introduced in

Grade 1 was built upon using a similar but higher-level technique in all the other grades.

Unfortunately, both of these professional development programs were discontinued when the district suspended the use of substitute teachers for all professional development offerings. Grade-level groups continued to work to implement the daily problem in mathematics, however. During their monthly grade-level meetings, teachers shared difficult problems and what their students had done with them. They brought samples of student work for others to examine and discuss, focusing on the way questions were phrased within the problems. They considered possible revisions that would produce higher-level questions. Along the way teachers were accumulating thought-provoking questions they could use with their students.

Throughout this time, the Data Team continued to meet about twice a month. The tasks before the team shifted to handling problems and monitoring progress within the grade-level groups. During these meetings, team members supported one another's efforts to move the school forward even though some of the strategies had to be adjusted and others eliminated. Since the strategies that had brought the entire school together were no longer in place, the required monthly grade-level meetings became a key component for ensuring that the entire school continued to focus on problem solving and faithful implementation of the mathematics curriculum.

Despite the implementation challenges and the adjustments that were made, the work produced results: The school's test scores for 2004–05 in mathematics problem solving improved from 59.9 to 67.5 percent (Joan Lombard, personal communication, 2006). Katz Elementary School joined other Using Data Project schools in celebrating their success at a gala celebration in the spring of 2005, where Using Data Project staff shared the findings from project evaluators that documented positive changes in school culture, collaboration, and data use.

Project Facilitator's Commentary

The implementation did not go quite as planned, but the school was still able to carry on even though the staff encountered what they deemed to be a major setback with the inability to use substitute teachers during their professional development sessions. The staff proved to be dedicated to the cause and came up with creative ways to find time to work and learn together. Team members strongly supported each other and, ultimately, the school as they continued to push forward with a focus on mathematics problem solving. While some monitoring was taking place through dialogue, I think this is one place that the team still needs to focus on more in their future work.

Principal's Commentary

Through this process we learned the importance of monitoring our progress continuously rather than just at the end as well as the importance of having resources to use for monitoring. We learned early on that we had few data sources that would allow us to look at student progress in the area of problem solving throughout the year and the importance of having such data sources. Through the Using Data Process we realized we needed, and th erefore we created, benchmark assessments that would allow us to examine student understanding along the way in order to make adjustments in instruction and continue to move forward. We believe these assessment tools will be invaluable as we continue to strive for improvement in learning for all students.

SUMMARY REFLECTIONS

The process of learning to engage in collaborative inquiry around data proved to take a bit longer than anyone thought it would, but it was time well spent. The Data Team worked steadily to learn how to use the different tools presented in the Using Data Toolkit (now part of *The Data Coach's Guide to Improving Learning for All Students*; Love, Stiles, Mundry, & DiRanna, 2008) and then shared that information with the staff through grade-level meetings or staff meetings.

While the team spent close to a year learning the process in a hands-on fashion, the time proved to be invaluable. In the fall of 2005, the Data Coaches put together a three-day Data Team retreat in which they worked through the entire process to determine student-learning problems, possible causes, and potential strategies. To help with this process, the Data Team was once again expanded to include two teachers per grade level to ensure that there would always be a grade-level representative at every data meeting regardless of track breaks.

Finally, the team has expanded its work with data from mathematics to all subject areas. Using the process to examine reading and writing, they have found that students seem to struggle in communicating their understanding of concepts that deal with higher-order thinking skills. It appears as though problem solving is not only an issue for students in mathematics, but a challenge in all areas. With that idea in mind, the team has decided to work on problem solving across the curricula in the hope that this will bring about long-term benefits for all students at Katz Elementary School. To better reflect its wider goal, the Data Team also changed its name and is now referred to as the School Improvement Team.

APPENDIX A: STUDENT WORK ON "ADDWORM" TASK

Name: Date:

The Addworm

This problem gives you the chance to

- *use simple rules*
- *complete a chart and look for patterns*
- *solve problems*

Many unusual animals live on the planet Htam.

Some of them have bodies that are made of cube shapes.

These animals grow by getting new cube shapes on each birthday.

When the Addworm is born it looks like this.

It is 1 cube long and it has 2 legs.

On its first birthday it looks like this.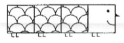

It is 4 cubes long and has 8 legs.

The Addworm continues to grow in this way.

On each birthday it gets 3 more cube shapes and 6 more legs.

Name: Date:

Now try to answer these questions about Addworms.
You may find it helpful to make Addworms using colored cubes.
Use some of the squares provided to draw each Addworm.

1. Draw a picture of an Addworm when it is 2 years old.

How long is it?   7 cubes long
How many legs does it have?   14 legs

2. Draw a picture of an Addworm when it is 3 years old.

How long is it?   10 cube long
How many legs does it have?   20 legs

3. How long is an Addworm when it is 6 years old? 19 cubes
How many legs does it have?   38 legs
You may wish to draw it.

Explain how you figured it out. _I filled in the cubes untill I had 3×6 cubes then I counted each leg by 2's._

4. Scientists are studying how Addworms grow. They have
collected some in their laboratory. One Addworm is 13 cubes
long. How old do you think it is? 4 in a half

(Continued)

(Continued)

Name:	Date:

5. Another Addworm has 32 legs. How old do you think it is? _5 years old_

Explain how you figured it out. _I added cubes so that I could see each cube had two legs. I counted each of legs until I got 32. Then I counted each 3 cubes as 1 year old and got my answers._

6. The scientists who are studying Addworms have begun to make this chart. Try to help them by filling in the empty spaces.

Age	Number of cubes long	Number of legs
at birth	1	2
1st birthday	4	8
2nd birthday	7	14
3rd birthday	10	20
4th birthday	13	26
5th birthday	16	32
6th birthday	19	38

7. Describe any number patterns you see in the chart.
The pattern I see is that in birthdays the age keeps getting 3 cubes. The leg pattern you x it with the number of cubes.

A Data Team Problem Solves About Problem Solving ● 159

Name:	Date:

8. Try to figure out the age of an Addworm when it is 28 cubes long. The number patterns in the chart may help you. Use a calculator if you wish. Explain how you figured it out.

I went back to the begiy of my paper and kept counting until I could get to 28. I didn't and had a cub left. As I counted the cubes again in threes this time and got 9. I thout for a while and tought that made the other cube stood for ½ so its 9½.

9. Try to figure out the age of an Addworm with 50 legs. The number patterns in the chart may help you. Use a calculator if you wish. Explain how you figured it out.

I drew a body of an addworm and mad 3 cubes for each year. I counted each cube by 20 until I got 50. Then I counted each cach 3 cubes again and got 8.

SOURCE: The Balanced Assessment Project, University of California, Berkeley. Reprinted with permission.

NOTE: This figure is also used in *The Data Coach's Guide to Improving Learning for All Students: Unleashing the Power of Collaborative Inquiry* (pp. 357–360), by N. Love, K. E. Stiles, S. Mundry, and K. DiRanna, 2008, Thousand Oaks, CA: Corwin Press.

APPENDIX B: TEACHER OBSERVATIONS OF STUDENT WORKING ON "ADDWORM" TASK

Name of Student: _____   Date: 6/10/04

Interviewer: Jones   Grade: 4

Say:
While you are working on this task, I will be working on my part of this assignment. On your own, I want you to work on this task and do your best at it. When you are finished, put your pencil down and turn your test over. Let's read page 1 together, follow along as I read. (Read up to question # 1. At that point, offer no more explanation. Take notes to describe student behavior/action while working.)

Observations:

Now try to answer these questions about Addworms.
You may find it helpful to make Addworms using colored cubes.
Use some of the squares provided to draw each Addworm.

1. Draw a picture of an Addworm when it is 2 years old.

   How long is it? _____
   How many legs does it have? _____

2. Draw a picture of an Addworm when it is 3 years old.

   How long is it? _____
   How many legs does it have? _____

3. How long is an Addworm when it is 6 years old? _____
   How many legs does it have? _____
   You may wish to draw it.

   Explain how you figured it out. _____

4. Scientists are studying how Addworms grow. They have collected some in their laboratory. One Addworm is 13 cubes long. How old do you think it is?

5. Another Addworm has 32 legs. How old do you think it is? _____

   Explain how you figured it out. _____

6. The scientists who are studying Addworms have begun to make this chart. Try to help them by filling in the empty spaces.

Age	Number of cubes long	Number of legs
at birth	1	2
1st birthday	4	8
2nd birthday		
3rd birthday		
4th birthday		
5th birthday		
6th birthday		

7. Describe any number patterns you see in the chart.
   _____
   _____

Asked about drawing pictures with cube
Looked back at beginning
Shaded cubes
Looked back again
answered question
wrote # of legs

began shading in cubes
pointed/counted cubes
answered
pointed/counted cubes
answered # of legs
began shading cubes
pointed/counted cubes
Shaded
pointed/counted cubes
Shaded.. pointed/counted
wrote answer
pointed/counted recounted
Wrote # legs - Looked
back at beginning - wrote
explanation - recounted

Wrote answer - shaded cubes
looked back at the beginning
erased answer - shaded more
cubes - recounted / pointed -
shaded 1 more - recounted
Wrote answer - erased - rewrote
Shaded all of Cubes - counted/pointed
cubes - recounted - erased 4 cubes -
recounted - wrote answer -
erased it - wrote answer
wrote explanation - erased part of
it - rewrote - erased beginning of
explanation - rewrote - erased
ending + rewrote

Filled in 8 cubes - erased
Wrote 7... wrote 14 legs
wrote 10 cubes - 13 cubes - 16-19-
wrote 20 legs - - wrote numbers
by 13 - wrote 26 - erased numb.
wrote # by 16 - wrote 32 - erased
#'s - math problem 19+19 -
wrote 38 legs - erased problem
looked over chart again after
writing explanations. Erased
part of explanation - rewrote

1. a Drawing it
   b. Went back to 1st page -
   1st - birthday has 4 cubes
   c. Putting 3 more cubes for
   each yr. / birthday.
   d. long pause - I did it this way
   because I thought it was the only
   way of my mind

2. a. Same way (after long pause)
   b. Filled them in until...
   each 3 cubes... until I
   have 3 of the 3 to make
   3 yrs. old.
   c. How could I keep adding 3
   when there was 4 in the 1st year.
   d. When it starts out it has 1
   cube - it gets 3 more -
   its confusing whether to add
   3 more for each year

3. a. Drawing it - I find it easier
   to draw it before doing it.
   b. I counted each 3 again
   for the year, I counted each
   cube having 2 legs,
   c. How to explain it.
   d. Because it's hard to explain
   the way to tell others, You know
   but you can't say it.

4. a. Drawing it again
   b. Then I thought what
   will I do with extra cube
   left over from each 3.
   c. That maybe the extra
   meant 1/2.
   d. Because there's an extra
   one y its the only thing on my
   mind I think it means.

5. a. Drawing it.
   b. I started to count each cube
   having 2 legs.
   c. How many cubes I would need
   to make 32 legs.
   d. Because that's how I thought
   of doing it.

6. a. Looking how many cubes
   at 1st y 2nd birthday
   b. adding 3 more to 4
   c. How should I try to find the
   number of legs. (TE - How did
   you do it?)
   d. timesing the number
   of cubes - 2 times

8. Try to figure out the age of an Addworm when it is 28 cubes long. The number patterns in the chart may help you. Use a calculator if you wish. Explain how you figured it out.

hesitated
looked back at beginning -
pointed /counted squares
Wrote explanation

8. Try to figure out the age of an Addworm with 50 legs. The number patterns in the chart may help you. Use a calculator if you wish. Explain how you figured it out.

worked problem off to side
50
50
50
150
wrote explanation
erased problem
Kept answer, wrote
150 ÷ 2

2X 50 = 300
300=100X3 *wrote wrote explanation new problem*
50+50 = 100
erased all problems + part of explanation, erased again + rewrote
Asked if she could draw on bottom. - Drew squares # after every 3 - recounted squares
drew square underneath
20 23-24- 26 - 25
28 30 34 40-50-60.

8. a. Went to front page - I counted 3 - until I got to 28 - I didn't I had a cube left.
b. I decided it was a half.
c. How to find out what 20 cubes showed how old an addworm was.
d. Because thats how I thought it.

9. a. Trying to 2 times 50.
b. Trying to figure out if 50+50 that you needed 100 cubes to have 50 legs.
c. I decided to draw the body of the add worm.
d. I thought if I drew it it would be easier to figure out.

Once the student has finished the test, say:
Now that you are finished with this task, let's talk about your work. I need to remember what you say, so I will be writing down exactly what you say.

Erased 30-31-33-36-39-4
new row.

Ask the following for each question:
erased all test
a. **Where did you start?** *1st row — recounted*
b. **What did you do next?**
c. **What were you thinking?** *add Squares to 8*
d. **Why?** *erased explanation - rewrote explanation*

SOURCE: From *The Data Coach's Guide to Improving Learning for All Students: Unleashing the Power of Collaborative Inquiry* (pp. 361–362), by N. Love, K. E. Stiles, S. Mundry, and K. DiRanna, 2008, Thousand Oaks, CA: Corwin Press. Reprinted with permission.

REFERENCES

Bloom, B. S. (1984). The search for methods of group instruction as effective as one-to-one tutoring. *Educational Leadership, 41*(8), 4–17.

Love, N., Stiles, K. E., Mundry, S., & DiRanna, K. (2008). *The data coach's guide to improving learning for all students: Unleashing the power of collaborative inquiry.* Thousand Oaks, CA: Corwin Press.

Final Thoughts

By Nancy Love

Things were pretty crazy, but at least nobody got killed today. So in truth, it was a good day.

—Principal in Boston area middle school

Recently, when I asked one of my friends, a principal at a middle school in the Boston area, "How was your day?" he responded: "Things were pretty crazy, but at least nobody got killed today. So in truth, it was a good day." He went on to explain that he had just discovered a "hit list"—a list of students that one unknown student in the school apparently was thinking about, or at least writing about, killing. The threat had to be taken seriously, as just a few weeks earlier a student was killed in a school in another nearby district. A good deal of this principal's focus for the next several weeks was taken up with a police investigation to prevent a possible murder or murders. My friend is a brilliant instructional leader committed to professional learning communities, yet he is spending his time just trying to keep the students in his school alive.

The conversation got me thinking about this monograph and the realities of schooling faced every day by educators like my friend. What relevance could this book possibly have for those simply struggling, on so many dimensions, for survival? What could we, the authors of the chapters in this book, tell my friend and others facing similar challenges that could actually make a difference? How can we even inch toward dramatic changes in school culture and student learning when many schools are in survival mode, just trying to get through another day?

HOW CAN WE IMPLEMENT COLLABORATIVE INQUIRY WHEN WE ARE IN SURVIVAL MODE?

Many educators find themselves walking a tightrope—struggling to find a balance between the urgencies of day-to-day demands and the important need to improve student learning, between complexity and coherence, external accountability and internal responsibility, the mundane and the moral. Some days, like the recent ones my friend has been experiencing, are just about maintaining a very precarious balance.

This book does not have simple answers to how to strike that balance. Some days, it is just one careful step at a time. What the monograph does offer is a compelling process—collaborative inquiry—for mobilizing the entire school community around the urgent and important business of improving student learning. Collaborative inquiry helps us find coherence in the complexity. It organizes a school community to act on the moral imperative, not just the external mandate to "leave no child behind." And perhaps most important, collaborative inquiry establishes a community of learners who walk together, providing a safety net for each other and for students. Collaborative inquiry is the place we are walking to: an established system of data-supported, collective problem solving and intervention in the face of complex challenges.

Start Small

As this monograph has shown, collaborative inquiry is big—nothing short of wholesale cultural change through long-term capacity building. Like any big change, it evolves over time. And though it is a flexible process that schools can engage in gradually, it is time-consuming, especially as educators first begin to learn it.

So if you have not already done so, how can you begin to move toward collaborative inquiry, lay the groundwork, or engage in aspects of it? Here are some possibilities for small steps you can take toward collaborative inquiry. I offer them in my closing thoughts not as the last word, but as a stimulus to your thinking about even more and better possibilities.

Some Suggestions for Teachers

- Experiment with your own teaching, using your own classroom data to inform your instructional improvement.
- Start up conversations with your colleagues about teaching and learning, sharing your successes, mistakes, and lessons learned and eliciting theirs.

- Meet with a few like-minded colleagues after school to strategize about how to get collaborative inquiry going in your school.
- Generate your own common assessments if none are available.
- Take advantage of daily conversations to say what you think is important and why.
- Share this book with key decision makers.
- Take on one part of the Using Data Process, such as Verifying Causes, or use one tool, such as Data-Driven Dialogue.
- Seek out professional development opportunities and resources to build your own knowledge and skill in collaborative inquiry.
- Make cultural proficiency a personal/professional growth priority: Put yourself in situations where you will interact with and learn from people whose culture is different than yours (e.g., go to different conferences, visit different neighborhoods, talk at length with your students and their families).
- Drill down into whatever data you have available.
- Request more relevant data to work with if little are currently available.

Some Suggestions for Principals

All of the above teachers' list after the second bullet, plus

- Grab whatever time there is—faculty meetings, professional development days—to engage in powerful conversations about teaching and learning.
- Model using data and cultural proficiency in your own practice.
- Make cultural proficiency a schoolwide priority and align practices and policies accordingly.
- Develop a multiyear plan for phasing in collaborative inquiry, starting with one Data Team and expanding from there.
- Share this book with key decision makers and your faculty, or use it as the basis for a study group.
- Schedule a summer data retreat for your staff.
- Provide professional development opportunities for teachers in key areas: data literacy and collaborative inquiry; content knowledge, generic pedagogical knowledge, and pedagogical content knowledge; cultural proficiency; and leadership and facilitation skills.
- Apply the lessons from the Clark County case (Chapter 6) to launch a schoolwide improvement process.

Some Suggestions for District Leaders

All of the above principals' list, plus

- Apply the lessons from the Johnson County case (Chapter 5) to launch a districtwide improvement process.

- Invest in professional development to build leadership and capacity among teachers and administrators.
- Set clear priorities for the district to manage innovation overload and keep the focus on results.
- Make cultural proficiency a districtwide priority and align practices and policies accordingly.

Think Big

As you consider what next steps might be best for your context and role, I want to return to the compelling moral imperative of this work and the overarching goal of this monograph: to turn the challenges of accountability into our greatest opportunity to prevent yet another generation of failure. The challenge, ultimately, is not accountability as measured by numbers or percentages on a test. The challenge is to be accountable for keeping our students alive, in the full sense of the word—alive with a love of learning, a sense of humanity and dignity, and aspirations and opportunities for a bright future, their spirits intact. The fact is that we care about data because we care about students. The data are only the means to the end, which is to offer every child the choice of life and hope. Data give us a way to face the facts, as brutal as they may be sometimes, and to have the creative discussions that lead to powerful actions. As Paulo Freire (1973) says, "Education is an act of love, and thus an act of courage. It cannot fear the analysis of reality or . . . avoid creative discussion" (p. 38).

In the end, that is what I want from this monograph: that it will inspire all of us to summon the courage and the love to search out and discover what we do not yet know about how to educate all of our children. Discovering the unknown, after all, is the spirit of inquiry. Data and research can guide us. Collaborative inquiry can provide a map. Cultural proficiency can open our eyes to our cultural biases and help us keep our commitment to serve all students in the forefront. The lessons and stories in this book can inform and inspire us. Our communities—our Data Teams, professional learning communities, and the broader community of educators, policymakers, parents, and children—can stimulate, support, and sustain us.

My greatest hope is that, using all of these resources, we take on this investigation into improving teaching and learning with the same rigor and sense of urgency with which my friend is taking on his: as if students' lives depend on it.

REFERENCES

Freire, P. (1973). *Education for critical consciousness.* New York: Continuum.

Index

CORWIN PRESS

The Corwin Press logo—a raven striding across an open book—represents the union of courage and learning. Corwin Press is committed to improving education for all learners by publishing books and other professional development resources for those serving the field of PreK–12 education. By providing practical, hands-on materials, Corwin Press continues to carry out the promise of its motto: **"Helping Educators Do Their Work Better."**

NSDC's purpose: Every educator engages in effective professional learning every day so every student achieves.

naesp™ National Association of Elementary School **Principals**

Serving All Elementary &
Middle Level Principals

The mission of the National Association of Elementary School Principals is to lead in the advocacy and support for elementary and middle level principals and other education leaders in their commitment for all children.

T E R C

Our Vision and Mission

We imagine a future in which learners from diverse communities engage in creative, rigorous, and reflective inquiry as an integral part of their lives. We see teachers and students alike as members of vibrant communities where questioning, problem solving, and experimentation are commonplace. Such communities focus on actual problems for which there are no simple solutions.

The mission of Research for Better Teaching is to build teacher, leader, and institutional capacity to promote and sustain increased student learning and achievement. This means . . .

Teachers will:

- communicate to all students that they can achieve at high levels
- help students to develop a positive academic identity
- use multiple sources of data to make decisions about teaching
- be reflective about their practice
- provide expert instruction in every classroom

Leaders will cultivate, support, and sustain expert instruction by:

- sharing a common language and concept system about teaching and learning with teachers
- creating professional communities that believe in continual improvement and engage in the study of teaching and learning
- distributing leadership throughout the organization
- developing structural mechanisms and resources that foster organizational effectiveness
- ensuring shared responsibility and accountability for student learning and achievement

RBT will dedicate its resources to rally the courage and commitment of schools and districts to ensure expert teaching in every classroom.